THE DALE EARNHARDT STORY

A ROUNDTABLE PRESS BOOK

ESPN BOOKS

HYPERION

CONTENTS

INTRO 1 2 3 4

5 6 7 8

A MAN SO LO

IT WAS EARLY, ABOUT 7 A.M. on race day at the Daytona 500. Dale Earnhardt had agreed to do a short, taped interview with me for our *SportsCenter* and *RPM2Day* shows. One problem: **HE WAS STILL ASLEEP.** Jeff Gordon saw me milling about outside The Intimidator's motor coach. Clearly I didn't want to disturb him, but the clock was ticking. I walked over to Gordon and explained my dilemma. If he were in my shoes, I asked, **WOULD HE WAKE UP EARNHARDT?** "I wouldn't," Gordon said, laughing.

That's what it was like to face Dale Earnhardt. His mere presence, his carefully crafted mystique, filled you with fear. There must be countless drivers who look back on those Sundays when they had the lead, when all they had to do was hold their line for a few more laps, but for some unknown reason they moved over and let Earnhardt through.

By the time I **MUSTERED THE COURAGE** to climb the steps to his motor coach, other drivers had gathered with Gordon to watch. I knocked on the door. Not terribly loud. Truth be told, I'd have called it a victory had I gotten no response. I'd made the effort. I had witnesses. I'd stood up to Dale Earnhardt.

Teresa Earnhardt answered the door. **I MUMBLED SOMETHING** about how Dale had agreed to an interview. She told me he was still sleeping. I believe I just stood there and endorsed sleep. "Sleep is great. I'd be sleeping too. One can't get enough sleep before a race."

GORDON AND THE OTHERS LAUGHED AT MY LAME ATTEMPT.

Before The Intimidator let me into his world, he put me in my place a second time. He'd just won the Daytona 500 after twenty years of trying. He and his entourage arrived at our studio. They may have consumed some champagne. As Earnhardt charged through the front door, he looked at me and asked, **"YOU STILL DATING JEFF GORDON?"**

THE ROOM FELL APART.

I had no response. **EARNHARDT WAS PUNISHING ME** for all the stories I'd done with NASCAR's new hot driver. He was either suggesting that I should have spread the television time around more evenly or he was **HAMMERING ME SIMPLY FOR SPORT,** I'm not sure which.

A year later at Daytona, ESPN invited him to cohost the show for a few days as the reigning 500 champion. After one show, Earnhardt asked if I wanted to come to dinner on his yacht. My answer, of course, was yes, but I hesitated in responding. **I WASN'T SURE IF HE WAS PUTTING ME ON.**

David Letterman flashed through my mind. Years before, I'd interviewed him at the Ed Sullivan Theater about his love for auto racing. As I was leaving, we crossed paths on the street. He yelled to my crew and me, "Hey, you wanna go out and get something to eat?" We said, "Sure." I took a few steps toward him to work out the plans. **LETTERMAN** got in his car and drove off.

Earnhardt's boat was the size of Bristol Motor Speedway. Dale, Teresa, and I were the only people on board. The couple asked me about my family and they were compassionate about the loss of my twin sons, Creighton and Connor. They showed me picture after picture of their children. We went through one photo album, then another. I was having trouble staying with the conversation because of a cold I'd been nursing. Now this might blow it for you forever, but Dale Earnhardt was my nurse that night. He offered a half-dozen remedies and way more counsel than an Intimidator should about fighting a cold. He almost sounded like a humble, caring person. He announced that he had to go to some kind of sponsor event, but he told me to sit and look through more photos with Teresa. **THIS WAS GETTING WEIRD.** The Intimidator was leaving, and I was supposed to stay on his yacht with his wife. Only then did he set the record straight. After saying good-bye, he turned to me and said, **"DON'T STAY TOO LONG."**

There are others who knew him far better than me. Others with better stories. In the short time I was around him, though, Dale Earnhardt delivered two of the funniest wisecracks I've ever heard. Each time, I was the butt of the joke, and I'm still laughing. When I think of him now, I don't see the crash into the wall. I don't care to see that image ever again. In my mind's eye, he's always in control. Of a race. Of a conversation. Of a room. I'm no longer intimidated by him. When a guy tries his damnedest to find you a cold remedy, when he lets you see him sipping red wine on a yacht while looking through photos of his kids, he stops being scary. But I guess T-shirt and hat sales might have suffered had he been known as **THE CONSIDERATE ONE.**

The black cap and sunglasses are fine by me. When I recall Dale Earnhardt, however, I think of other things, things that make me smile. The pictures I remember most are those taken right after his Daytona 500 win. In general, postrace celebrations are small. Only the people on the winning team join in. Everyone else commiserates over what might have been. Earnhardt's victory party was different. As he drove **THE 3 CAR** onto pit road, **A SEA OF PEOPLE FLOWED TO HIS SIDE**, as if all forty-three pit crews had worked for him that day. One by one, the crew members reached out their hands to touch him in a show of admiration and respect. I'm sure it's hard for the guys in car racing to admit, **BUT INTIMIDATOR IS A FUNNY WAY TO DESCRIBE A MAN SO LOVED.**

YOU
CAN'T
PUT

CHAPTER

IN YOU

RALPH EARNHARDT WAS ALWAYS THE MOVING FORCE BEHIND HIS SON.

YOU CAN'T PUT IT IN YOU

DALE EARNHARDT LIKED TO TELL A STORY ABOUT A LONG-FORGOTTEN RACE ON THE RED CLAY TRACK AT THE METROLINA FAIRGROUNDS IN CHARLOTTE. THIS WAS BACK IN 1972. DALE WAS NEW TO THE SPORT. HE WAS DRIVING A SIX-CYLINDER SEMIMODIFIED IN NASCAR'S SPORTSMAN DIVISION. HIS FATHER, RALPH, WAS RUNNING WITH THE MORE EXPERIENCED GRAND NATIONAL CROWD. ON THIS FRIDAY NIGHT, THE FIELD AT METROLINA WAS SMALL, SO THE TRACK'S PROMOTERS INVITED YOUNG DALE AND A HANDFUL OF OTHER SEMIMODIFIED DRIVERS TO JOIN THE HUNT. IT WAS THE ONLY TIME THAT FATHER AND SON SHARED THE SAME TRACK.

Late in the race, Ralph was leading the pack. Dale was running fourth. He did not have enough car to pass the drivers in front of him. He was so far off the lead, in fact, that Ralph appeared in Dale's rearview mirror, all but kissing his son's bumper. Fully expecting to be lapped, Dale moved over. Ralph moved with him. Nosing up to Dale's tail end, the ever-resourceful father pushed his son into third place, past another semimodified driver. The poor guy could do nothing but grumble, "Those damn Earnhardts!"

This story might well be apocryphal, but it's true in spirit: Ralph Earnhardt was always the moving force behind his son. He was not an educated man. He had dropped out of school in the sixth grade. Like most everyone in the small North Carolina town of Kannapolis, he worked for a stretch in the Cannon Mills, just another so-called lint head in the textile trade. To supplement his income, he also labored in a local garage, rebuilding taxicab engines for the city. When a colleague of his began building a dirt racer, Ralph lent him a hand. Once the car was complete, the colleague let Ralph drive it in a few races. He was off and running.

In the 1950s, stock car racing was one of the fastest-growing sports in rural America. It seemed like every town in North Carolina had its own dirt track. A hustling driver could find a race pretty much any night of the week. Monday in Asheville, Tuesday in Greensboro, Thursday in Columbia, Sunday in Concord. A loosely structured governing body called the National Association of Stock Car Racing kept an eye on things, but nobody really kept records. Each track managed its own business. The only constant was this: the first driver across the finish line got the prize money. Long before the advent of career rankings and statistics, Ralph Earnhardt earned himself a legacy as one of the finest drivers of his day.

OPPOSITE // FUTURE MOTORSPORTS HALL OF FAME DRIVER RALPH EARNHARDT DOMINATED NORTH CAROLINA SHORT-TRACK RACING IN CARS HE BUILT IN THE GARAGE BEHIND HIS HOUSE.

YOU CAN'T PUT IT IN YOU

HE LIVED TO RACE AND RACED TO LIVE

// ESPN BUILT SEVEN REPLICA CARS FOR THE MOVIE 3, AMONG THEM RALPH EARNHARDT'S "GO OR BLOW."

"WHEN HE FIRST TOLD ME HE WAS GOING TO QUIT HIS JOB AND RACE," HIS WIFE MARTHA ONCE SAID, "I THOUGHT, WELL, HE'S LOST HIS MIND.

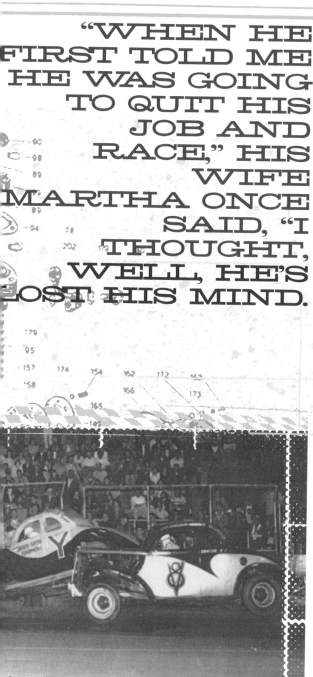

I threatened to leave him but he just kept talking. He promised me that if he couldn't do it without taking away from the family he would quit. He always kept me and the five kids up without me having to work, so I couldn't say too much."

In the garage out in back of the house, Ralph built and serviced his cars. It's fair to claim that the Dale Earnhardt legend was born in that well-oiled space between the engines and the hoods. As soon as the boy could walk, he was shadowing his father. He performed hour upon hour of scut work before Ralph let him pick up a wrench. There in the shop, father and son discovered their shared passion. Only a spin on the racetrack could beat it. It's no wonder that Dale's earliest memory involved Ralph racing one of those cars. As he recalled, he was standing in the bed of a truck watching his father leading the pack.

Ralph Earnhardt's philosophy was simple: competitors might outrun him, but they sure as heck weren't going to outwork him. He built his own chassis and his own engines. He knew every bolt in every car he drove. If he could not guarantee himself the fastest ride at the start of a race, he made damn certain that he would be motoring along at the finish.

And Dale was with him every step of the way. People in Kannapolis used to say, "If you weren't looking at Ralph's crankcase, you didn't get to know Dale." He was a whole lot more interested in learning how to build a carburetor with his father than learning how to solve math problems. "I can remember sitting in school, counting the seconds ticking off the clock until I could get home and help him in the shop," he said. On weeknights, when he couldn't go to the track with his father, Dale would creep from his bedroom at dawn to inspect Ralph's car. The dirt and the dents told him everything he needed to know. "All I had to do was look at the front end," Dale explained. "If the front end was pretty clean that meant he had a good race and probably won."

ABOVE // RALPH EARNHARDT GENERALLY DROVE CAUTIOUSLY TO PRESERVE HIS EQUIPMENT—BUT WHEN NECESSARY HE WOULDN'T HESITATE TO SWAP PAINT.

RALPH ZIPPED UP AND DOWN THE EAST COAST FOUR OR FIVE NIGHTS A WEEK, SOMETIMES WINNING THREE OR FOUR RACES. IN SHORT ORDER, HE DEVELOPED A REPUTATION AS THE MAN TO BEAT. LEGEND HAS IT HE WAS BANNED FROM THE TRACK IN HICKORY, NORTH CAROLINA, FOR A SEASON BECAUSE HE WON TOO OFTEN AND TOO EASILY. PEOPLE STOPPED BUYING TICKETS.

YOU CAN'T PUT IT IN YOU

THEREAFTER, RALPH MADE A PRACTICE OF HANGING BACK UNTIL THE MAD RUSH TO THE CHECKERED FLAG. "THERE'S ONLY ONE LAP YOU NEED TO LEAD," HE TAUGHT HIS SON, "AND THAT'S THE LAST LAP." IN 1956, RALPH WON THE LATE MODEL SPORTSMAN DIVISION CHAMPIONSHIP. IN 1997, HE WAS INDUCTED INTO THE INTERNATIONAL MOTORSPORTS HALL OF FAME. A YEAR LATER, HE WAS NAMED ONE OF THE FIFTY GREATEST DRIVERS IN NASCAR HISTORY.

YOU CAN'T PUT IT IN YOU

// ONLY THE DIRT WAS REAL IN THIS MOVIE RECREATION.

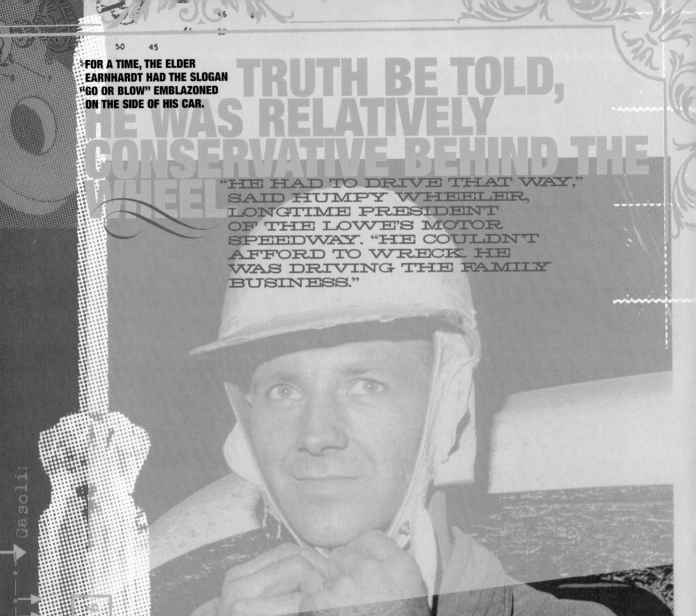

FOR A TIME, THE ELDER EARNHARDT HAD THE SLOGAN "GO OR BLOW" EMBLAZONED ON THE SIDE OF HIS CAR.

TRUTH BE TOLD, HE WAS RELATIVELY CONSERVATIVE BEHIND THE WHEEL.

"HE HAD TO DRIVE THAT WAY," SAID HUMPY WHEELER, LONGTIME PRESIDENT OF THE LOWE'S MOTOR SPEEDWAY. "HE COULDN'T AFFORD TO WRECK. HE WAS DRIVING THE FAMILY BUSINESS."

YOU CAN'T PUT IT IN YOU

In the days before GM Goodwrench and Budweiser joined the fun, a guy like Ralph could only collect a few bucks here and there by painting a sponsor's name on the side of a car, much like those Little League coaches who are beholden to mom-and-pop stores for uniforms. "My Daddy did a lot with a little," said Dale, who later inherited Ralph's primary sponsor, Dainty Maid Food Products. But what Ralph lacked in money, he more than made up in ingenuity. Consider, for example, the screwdriver story. Back when Ralph was racing, NASCAR once instituted a slight engine modification that resulted in a slew of broken axle keys. Small part, big problem. According to Earnhardt biographer Leigh Montville, Ralph discovered the solution by replacing his keys with the shaft of a number 6 screwdriver. He then made the most of his discovery by purchasing nearly every number 6 screwdriver in the state.

This way of thinking was not lost on Dale. As a child, he burned with the desire to win at everything. "Losing just isn't part of the plan," he exclaimed. The first trophy he brought home was for a victory in slot car racing. He also humbled the neighborhood boys on the seat of his home-made bicycle—sometimes riding backwards to make things more interesting. When he was old enough to set foot on the local tracks, his father built him a go-kart. As a teenager, he got yet another taste of victory by working on his father's pit crew.

AS A CHILD, HE BURNED WITH THE DESIRE TO WIN AT EVERYTHING.

IRON

THOSE WHO KNEW RALPH DESCRIBED HIM AS FOCUSED AND SERIOUS. THEY MARVELED AT HIS INNER CALM. MINUTES AFTER A RACE, IT WAS IMPOSSIBLE TO TELL FROM THE MAN'S DEMEANOR IF HE HAD WON OR PILED UP. APTLY NICK-NAMED "IRONHEART," RALPH WAS NOT GIVEN TO GRAND DISPLAYS OF EMOTION. HE PREFERRED TO KEEP HIS FEELINGS TO HIMSELF. EVERY WORD HE UTTERED COUNTED FOR SOMETHING. "YOU KNEW HE LOVED YOU," SAID HIS SON, "BUT HE DIDN'T SAY THAT. HE DIDN'T SAY HE LOVED YOU ALL THE TIME. I KNEW HE LOVED US BY THE WAY HE PROVIDED FOR US AND THE THINGS HE DID FOR ME WHEN I WAS A CHILD."

HEART

IN THE END, RALPH WAS A PROUD MAN WHO NEVER FELT THE NEED TO BRAG ABOUT HIS ACCOMPLISHMENTS.

HE DID WHAT HE NEEDED TO DO WHEN IT NEEDED TO BE DONE.

He wanted a better life for his two daughters and his three sons. That's what all those late nights in the garage were all about. After dropping out of school, he learned the value of an education.

CLOCKWISE FROM UPPER LEFT // MARTHA AND RALPH; DALE (AT LEFT) WITH YOUNGER BROTHERS RANDY AND DANNY; AND THE YOUNG INTIMIDATOR.

DALE IDOLIZED HIS FATHER, SO MUCH SO THAT, WHEN HE WAS SIXTEEN YEARS OLD, A FRESHMAN IN HIGH SCHOOL, HE ANNOUNCED THAT HE WAS THROUGH WITH CLASSWORK. NO USE ARGUING, HE WAS GOING TO BE A STOCK CAR RACER.

RALPH AND MARTHA WERE OUTRAGED.

THEY TRIED TO BRIBE THEIR SON WITH A NEW CAR. DALE WOULD HAVE NONE OF IT. "WHEN DALE GOT IN THE RACE CAR," SAID HIS MOTHER, "THAT WAS JUST ALTOGETHER DIFFERENT FROM HIS FATHER. I GREW UP WITH RALPH RACING AND I KNEW HE KNEW WHAT HE WAS DOING. WHEN DALE GOT IN IT, THAT WAS A PART OF ME GETTING IN THAT CAR AND IT WAS JUST A DIFFERENT STORY." RALPH WAS SO UPSET HE STEWED FOR CLOSE TO A YEAR AND A HALF. HE DID NOT WANT DALE TO LIVE THE LIFE HE HAD, SHUTTLING FROM RACE TO RACE, ALWAYS ONE WRECK AWAY FROM THE POORHOUSE. SATURDAY NIGHT SHOWDOWNS WITH $500 PURSES WERE NO WAY TO RAISE A FAMILY. MANY YEARS LATER, DALE WOULD ALSO COME TO REGRET THE DECISION. "IF I COULD DO ONE THING OVER," HE TOLD A REPORTER, "I'D STAY IN SCHOOL."

// FOR A BRIEF SPELL IN THE 1970S, DALE'S CAR SPORTED RALPH'S NUMBER 8.

ULTIMATELY, HOWEVER, IT WAS RALPH WHO PROVIDED HIS SON WITH A MASTER'S DEGREE IN HIS CHOSEN PROFESSION. BEFORE HE PASSED AWAY ON SEPTEMBER 26, 1973, WHILE TENDING TO A CARBURETOR IN THE GARAGE, HE BEQUEATHED TO DALE THE LESSONS OF A LIFETIME IN THE DRIVER'S SEAT. IT WASN'T SO MUCH THE NUTS-AND-BOLTS KNOWLEDGE THAT LED TO HIS SON'S SUCCESS, BUT RATHER THE EARNHARDT ETHIC: HARD WORK, CONFIDENCE, INGENUITY, RESPECT FOR THE COMPETITION, PRIDE IN EVERYTHING YOU DO. RALPH WAS AN EXEMPLARY TEACHER, BUT DALE WAS A TRULY GIFTED STUDENT. THAT MUCH WAS CLEAR FROM THE START. AS RALPH HIMSELF LIKED TO SAY,

"YOU CAN'T PUT IT IN YOU." THE BOY WAS A NATURAL

TALES OF THE DEMONIC

DRIVER

AS LONG AS THEY'RE RACING ONE AUTO-MOBILE AGAINST ANOTHER IN THIS COUNTRY, THEY WILL TELL THE STORIES. THE TALES OF THE DEMONIC DRIVER AND HIS BLACK MACHINE, A CHEVY WITH A FRONT BUMPER MADE OF IRON AND A REAR BUMPER THAT MEASURED TWENTY FEET WIDE. THEY WILL DESCRIBE THE TONGUES OF FLAME THAT BELCHED FROM HIS HEADER PIPES AND THE THUNDERBOLTS THAT RUMBLED FORTH FROM HIS ENGINE TO RATTLE THE BONES OF THOSE WHO DARED TO STAND IN HIS WAY. WITH THE PASSAGE OF TIME, THE CLAIMS WILL UNDOUBTEDLY GROW TALLER, BUT THEIR VALIDITY MUST NEVER BE QUESTIONED. FOR NO CLAIM IS TOO OUT-LANDISH WHEN IT COMES TO THE INTIMIDATOR.

"WHEN FANS MEET ME IN PERSON," DALE EARNHARDT ONCE RECALLED, "THEY ARE SURPRISED THAT I'M NOT TEN FEET TALL AND BULLETPROOF.

WELL, I'VE GOT BAD NEWS FOR EVERYBODY OUT THERE. I'M NOT. I'M ABOUT NINE FOOT SIX."

// THE INTIMIDATOR AT DAYTONA BEFORE THE START OF THE 1980 FIRECRACKER 500.

They talk of his last victory, the time when he defied physics and went from eighteenth to first in less than five laps to win at Talladega. Or the time when he so cleanly threaded a rapidly shrinking two-car needle at Bristol that the ESPN switchboard was locked up with viewers demanding more replays. Or the time that he psyched out an entire garage of Ford teams during a test session in Atlanta by parking his car and napping in the cockpit in plain view of his thrashing rivals. "I looked over at him sleeping there," recalled Robin Pemberton, crew chief for championship hopeful Mark Martin, "and I thought to myself, *we're screwed.*"

NASCAR dads forever tell their children of the night in 1995 when The Man in Black failed to win the race at Bristol, but left Thunder Valley with a much more important victory in the fight. Earnhardt had spun Rusty Wallace at the beginning of the race and Terry Labonte at the finish. Labonte rolled into Victory Lane with a memento from the second-place car painted onto his rear bumper and a front end pushed back nearly into his lap. Wallace confronted Earnhardt by tossing a water bottle at his head. The Intimidator simply smirked and winked.

"YOURS IS COMING!" WALLACE SHOUTED AS THE TWO WERE SEPARATED BY A MOB OF CREWMEN AND MEDIA MEMBERS. **THE THREAT WAS**

NOTHING NEW.

"RUBBIN' IS RACING"

For nearly three decades, Earnhardt's rivals—and even a handful of his friends—had vowed revenge as they stared into his wraparound sunglasses. None dared to follow through. Not even once. Perhaps it was the power of the legend that kept them from doing so. But, more than likely, it was the power of the man, the one who refused to spend his spare time on the golf course, opting instead to knock down trees and rearrange hillsides with his bulldozer, the one who turned heads when he entered a room even by way of the backdoor.

"He was always in control," says onetime rival and eventual friend, Darrell Waltrip. "He drove you crazy if you were driving to dinner. 'Turn here, speed up, slow down, watch where you're going.' And he did the same on the track. We'd be in a big pack at Daytona and his hands would be flying all over the place, 'You go here, you go there, get in behind me and we'll go.' It drove us all nuts, but we ended up pretty much doing what he told us to."

After a run-in with Earnhardt during an IROC race at Daytona, Indy 500 champion Eddie Cheever sat in his Pontiac Firebird awaiting his whipping. "He walked over to my car and everyone crowded around it just took a step back and got ready to watch me get my butt kicked," Cheever recounted. "He grabbed me with those giant hands and said, 'Don't do that s—t again.' That was it. I still haven't exhaled."

HISTORY DOES NOT DESIGNATE A SPECIFIC MOMENT FOR THE BIRTH OF THE INTIMIDATOR, BUT MOST BELIEVE THAT IT TOOK PLACE AT THE CHARLOTTE MOTOR SPEEDWAY ON MAY 17, 1997.

In the ninety-mile Winston All-Star Event, the kind of quick-blast match-race shootout that Earnhardt loved, the thirty-six-year-old driver bullied his way past NASCAR's best. He picked off the legendary likes of Petty and Allison, Yarborough and Labonte, muscling his way around Geoff Bodine into second place. When an angry Bill Elliott tried to turn Dale's car into a lawn mower, Earnhardt simply left the asphalt and cruised ahead into the lead—The Pass in the Grass.

Before that galvanizing moment, Earnhardt had ruffled rivals mostly with his brash driving skills. As a youngster he had barreled his way around the track as if every lap were a dash to the finish, eager to put a bumper to the demigods of the day. After stunning the grandstands with a gutsy win in the 1980 Busch Clash All-Star Event at Daytona, he awed them further by uttering stock car blasphemy. "There might be a trick or two that Richard Petty and Bobby Allison haven't shown me yet," he announced, "but I know I'm as good as they are."

As Petty told an ESPN reporter in 1999, "He was one of those that when you saw him coming, you braced yourself. You knew that if he didn't calm down, he wasn't going to make it. But you also knew that if he ever got all that talent and attitude harnessed, he was going to be pretty darn good."

Blend T-11 T-10

"IF HE DON'T GET HURT," CREW CHIEF JAKE ELDER SAID AFTER THE DRIVER'S FIRST CAREER WIN AT BRISTOL ON APRIL 1, 1979, "I THINK HE'S GOT AT LEAST TWELVE GOOD YEARS AHEAD OF HIM."

Over the next few seasons, Earnhardt managed to stand toe-to-toe with the stars of his sport, despite piloting an inferior craft. After drifting from ride to ride early in the decade, he landed with Richard Childress Racing for good in 1984. One year later, all bets were off… so were the gloves. In March, he shoved Ricky Rudd out of the way to win at Bristol. In August, he stiff-armed Waltrip and Tim Richmond on the same track, drawing howls of criticism from both. At Martinsville in September, he booted Richmond again. "I guess NASCAR thinks that overaggressive driving sells tickets," Waltrip said, his hands shaking from anger. When asked for an example of said driving, he simply pointed to the number 3 Wrangler Chevy in Victory Lane. "Y'all know who to watch if that's what you want to see."

TAKING A CUE FROM THE 1985 CHAMP, NASCAR'S FANS VOICED THEIR DISAPPROVAL, TOO. HOW DARE EARNHARDT DISRESPECT HIS ELDERS, HOW DARE HE WRECK OTHERS TO WIN. THEY SHOWERED HIM WITH BOOS—AND BOOZE—AT EVERY TURN. BUT AS THE INTIMIDATOR PILED UP WINS, THE SENTIMENT BEGAN TO CHANGE.

HECKLES GAVE WAY TO CHEERS, BOOS BECAME REBEL YELLS,

AND WHAT WAS ONCE SEEN AS AGGRESSION SUDDENLY MORPHED INTO AN UPLIFTING EXAMPLE OF THE WORKING MAN FIGHTING FOR ALL HE COULD GET.

"NO ONE GIVES YOU ANYTHING IN THIS LIFE," EARNHARDT SAID. "SO THAT MEANS THAT YOU HAVE TO GO OUT THERE AND MAKE IT HAPPEN FOR YOURSELF, ON THE RACE-TRACK OR AT WORK OR ANYWHERE."

NOW THAT THE CONGREGATION WAS BAPTIZED,

the Pass in the Grass became but one small highlight in an eleven-win season that ended with Winston Cup Championship number three. When Earnhardt returned to the track the following February, "Wrangler" was replaced by "GM Goodwrench" on the hood. The UCLA yellow and blue had yielded to Oakland Raider silver and black.

"When he rolled that car onto the track at Daytona for the Busch Clash in '88, people gasped," recalls Humpy Wheeler. "Now he didn't just drive mean, he *looked* mean. And he won that race going away. Here he was with that mustache and those mirrored sunglasses and that perpetually dirty face. And he only seemed to smile when he had muscled his way to a win. We officially had ourselves a new folk hero."

"WE OFFICIALLY HAD OURSELVES A NEW FOLK HERO."

HERO

Earnhardt dominated on short and intermediate tracks, but it was his mastery of the high-speed aerodynamic draft on the big ovals that left rivals eating his invisible wake. Other drivers needed a partner to seize hold of this magic. Earnhardt summoned it all on his own. With tiny adjustments to the position of his car, he created solo slipstreams and phantom bursts of power. He won a record ten races at Talladega. He won three times as much at Daytona. The victories, the moves, the passes . . . there was only one logical explanation. "The man could see the air," says Dale Jarrett with slack-jawed submission. "He denied it, but I saw him do things that proved it."

And yet Earnhardt's decisive genius was not limited to mastering the molecules around his car. Every move he made as a driver seemed to come to him as naturally as walking or breathing. He never surrendered control. Never wasted time trying to find the edge of the envelope. He just *knew.* How? One part bloodline, one part muscle, ninety-eight parts God-gifted talent.

"He is the last seat-of-the-pants racer," Andy Petree, crew chief for Earnhardt's sixth and seventh titles, said with amazement in 1995. "We're all changing shocks and springs and tires and adjusting on the car. But in the end, he had the ability to will that car to do whatever the hell he wanted it to do. If it was loose, he drove around it. If it was tight, he drove around it. He just knew how to do it. Some people are born to be politicians or painters or whatever. Dale was born to be a race car driver, plain and simple."

Before Earnhardt was The Intimidator, people called him Ironhead, survivor of mishaps that made eyewitnesses wince. During his rookie season, he walked away from a collarbone-smashing wreck at Pocono that looked like a plane had crashed on the backstretch. Three years later he broke his knee at Pocono. He was back to race one week later. At Talledega in 1996, he turned his Chevy over on the front stretch, smashing his collarbone yet again. He climbed from the car and waved to the crowd. Two weeks later, he won the pole at Watkins Glen, fully intending to surrender his ride to a backup driver. Earnhardt changed his mind, leading fifty-four laps and finishing sixth.

While vacationing on the coast of North Carolina, a motor sports writer walked up to a crowd listening to the race on a giant boom box. "What's happening at Watkins Glen?"

A man who looked to be in his fifties spoke up, tears welling in his eyes. "He's not getting out of the car. Know why? Because he's made of iron, that's why."

"HE IS THE LAST SEAT-OF-THE-PANTS RACER"

IN 1997, EARNHARDT ONCE MORE PULLED HIMSELF FROM A BATTERED MONTE CARLO AT DAYTONA. WHILE SITTING IN THE AMBULANCE, HE NOTICED THAT OLD NUMBER 3 HAD FOUR FUNCTIONING TIRES. "WILL THAT CAR STILL CRANK?" HE SHOUTED TO A MEMBER OF THE SAFETY CREW. YOU BET. EARNHARDT STOOD UP, CLIMBED BACK INSIDE THE COCKPIT, AND STARTED RACING. AS THE SHORTENED CHEVY ROLLED PAST THE GRANDSTANDS, THE ROAR FROM THE CROWD SURPASSED THAT RESERVED FOR JEFF GORDON, THE RACE'S EVENTUAL WINNER.

THAT IS WHY NASCAR NATION IS COVERED IN BLACK. WHY SLANTED 3S FLY FROM FLAGPOLES FROM THE CAROLINAS TO CALIFORNIA. WHY WORKING MEN AND WOMEN STILL LOOK TO DALE EARNHARDT FOR THE INSPIRATION THEY NEED TO PLUG THEIR WAY THROUGH THE THIRD SHIFT.

For thirty years, race fans asked only two questions on Sunday afternoons: **Who won?** and **Where did Earnhardt finish?** He was the show, plain and simple.

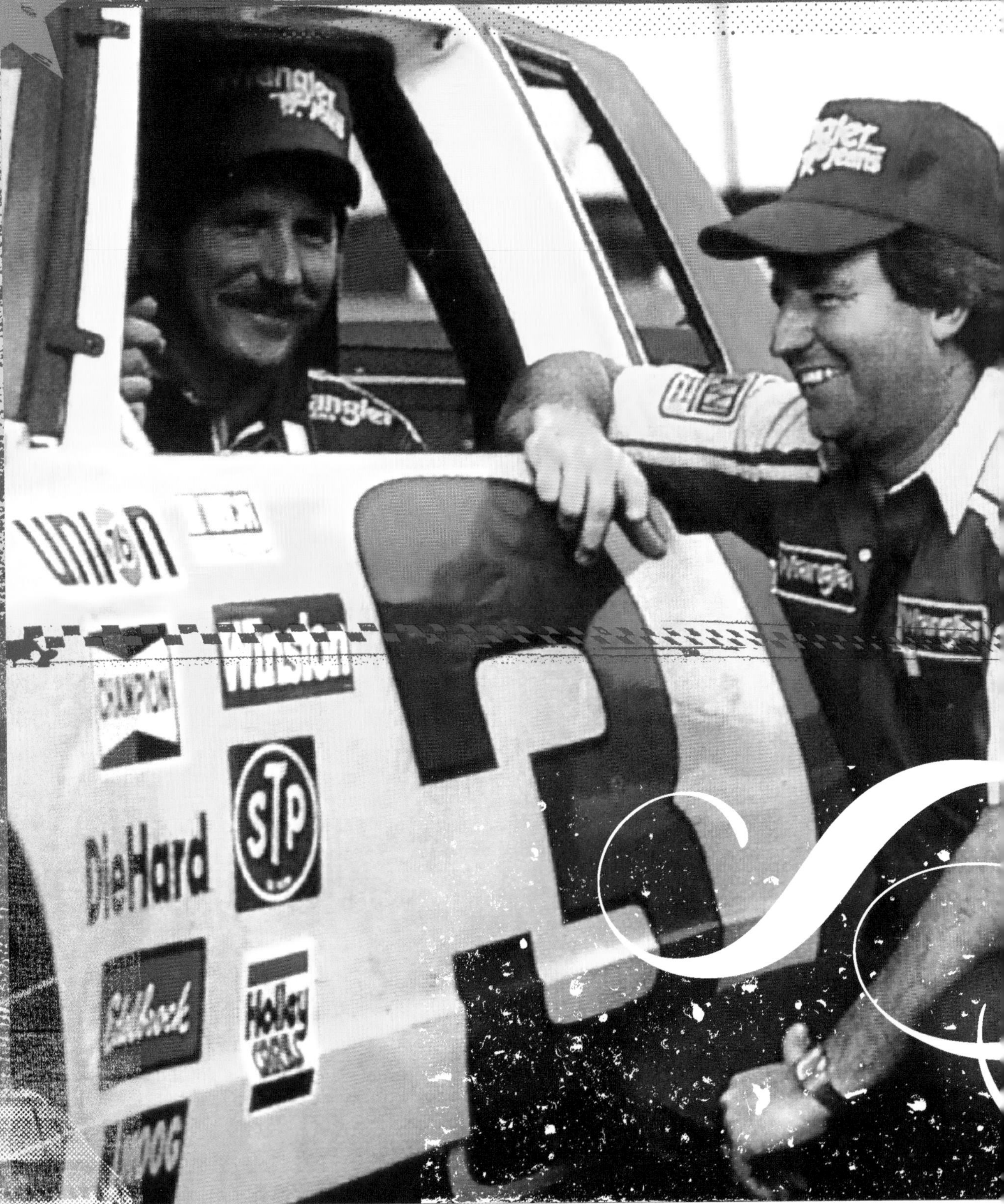
Winston
CHAMPION
STP
DieHard
Holley

DALE
NEVER STOPPED TO CONSIDER THE DYNAMICS OF THEIR RELATIONSHIP

THE BIG RED MACHINE. SHOWTIME. AMERICA'S TEAM. THE GREAT SPORTS DYNASTIES OF OUR TIME HAVE HAD ONE CHARACTER TRAIT IN COMMON—A MIND-BENDING CHEMISTRY THAT COULD SCOOP UP A ROOMFUL OF EGOS AND WHIP THEM INTO A SINGLE-PURPOSE ENGINE. BUT DALE EARNHARDT AND RICHARD CHILDRESS NEVER STOPPED TO CONSIDER THE DYNAMICS OF THEIR RELATIONSHIP. THEY WERE TOO DAMN BUSY.

"You reach a point with a race team where it is just automatic," Childress told *SportsCenter* in 1995. "No one has any doubts about what their job is or what they need to do. No one doubts that the outcome will be anything less than success because they just expect it. You just put your head down and go. The winning just happens."

For Dale and R.C., winning "just happened" more frequently than it had for any team in NASCAR's modern era. Six Winston Cup titles, sixty-seven race wins, twenty-two pole positions, and only one finish outside of the annual top-ten rankings in seventeen tries. Richard Childress Racing had the best driver, the best cars, and the best crew. These facts were understood by every man on the team and, more significantly, by every man who dared to challenge it.

"I HEARD
JACK NICKLAUS SAY SOMETHING ONE TIME,
AND IT COULD HAVE BEEN ABOUT US," SAYS KIRK SHELMERDINE,
CREW CHIEF OF THE NUMBER 3 CHEVY FROM 1984 TO 1992 AND
FOUNDING FATHER OF THE LEGENDARY FLYING ACES PIT CREW.

"**HE SAID** THAT BEFORE HE EVEN ARRIVED AT THE GOLF COURSE HE KNEW HE HAD ALL BUT A COUPLE OF GUYS BEAT BECAUSE THEY KNEW HE WAS BETTER THAN THEY WERE AND HE KNEW THAT THEY KNEW HE WAS BETTER THAN THEY WERE. THAT'S EXACTLY HOW WE WALKED INTO THAT GARAGE EVERY WEEKEND. AND IT STARTED WITH RICHARD AND DALE."

THE ART OF SELF-PROMOTION.

PUSHING THE INTIMIDATOR PHILOSOPHY

TO THE TOP OF THE POINT STANDINGS AND THE NEWLY TRADEMARKED SLANTED 3 TO THE TOP OF THE MERCHANDISE SALES LIST. BY THE TIME THEIR RUN WAS OVER, EVERY OTHER RACE TEAM WAS GREEN WITH ENVY AND THE FANS IN THE STANDS WERE SHELLING OUT THE GREEN TO CLOAK THEMSELVES IN BLACK. BLUE-COLLAR AMERICA FELT AN INSTANT BOND WITH THE TEAM'S OIL-COVERED HISTORY. THE CORPORATE GIANTS RECOGNIZED THIS PIPELINE AND BEFORE LONG CAME BEGGING FOR FIVE MINUTES WITH DALE AND R.C., FROM GENERAL MOTORS TO BURGER KING TO COCA-COLA. NOT BAD FOR A COUPLE OF GUYS WITH GREASY FINGERNAILS AND NARY A COLLEGE DIPLOMA BETWEEN THEM.

3 *Dale Earnhardt*

WINSTON CUP CHAMPIONS

1980   1986   1987   1990   1991
1993   1994

Snap-on   FOOD CITY   **RCR** *Richard Childress Racing Enterprises, Inc.*

RICHARD CHILDRESS HAD BEEN
A DRIVER HIMSELF. FOR THE
BETTER PART OF TWELVE
YEARS, HE LOADED UP HIS
SELF-CONSTRUCTED RACE CARS
AND TOWED THEM TO TRACKS
ALL OVER THE COUNTRY.

12 years

Richard Childress in the No. 3 CRC Chemicals car in

HE BUILT HIS OWN ENGINES, SHAPED HIS OWN SHEET METAL, AND PAID HIS OWN BILLS, DARING TO RACE AS AN INDEPENDENT AGAINST THE DETROIT FACTORY-FUNDED POWERHOUSES OF PETTY AND WOOD. *IN 285 CAREER STARTS, HE MANAGED ONLY SIX TOP-TEN EFFORTS, NEVER FINISHING HIGHER THAN THIRD.*

CAREER STARTS

285

6

HIGHEST FINISH

3

BUT BEFORE DAYTONA

AND DARLINGTON, THERE WERE BOWMAN GRAY, HICKORY, AND DOZENS OF OTHER TINY TRACKS DOTTING THE NORTH CAROLINA COUNTRYSIDE, DIRT PILES CHRISTENED YEARS EARLIER BY A SHORT-TRACK LEGEND NAMED RALPH EARNHARDT.

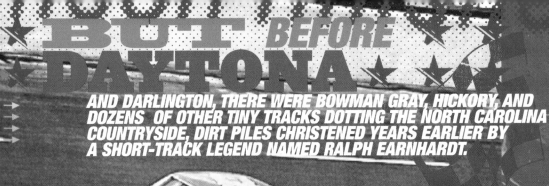

IN 1981,

// EARNHARDT AND CHILDRESS RACED SEVERAL CARS SPONSORED BY WRANGLER BEFORE FINALLY RACING INTO HISTORY IN THE BLACK GM GOODWRENCH NUMBER 3.

WHEN RALPH'S SON WAS SUDDENLY LEFT WITHOUT A RIDE,

CHILDRESS, THE LONGTIME OWNER-DRIVER, FOUND HIMSELF STANDING AT A CROSSROADS. DID HE CONTINUE TO TAKE HOLD OF THE WHEEL, OR DID HE HAND OVER THE KEYS TO THE RUGGED KID WITH THE PROVEN BLOODLINE?

HE DIDN'T STAND THERE LONG.

"DALE

HAD JUST WON HIS FIRST CHAMPIONSHIP THE YEAR BEFORE AND THEN THERE HE WAS WITHOUT A RIDE," CHILDRESS RECALLED IN 2001. "AND I HAD BEEN STRUGGLING WITH WHETHER OR NOT TO STOP DRIVING ANYWAY. BUT I KNEW DALE WAS ONE OF THE BEST RAW TALENTS THAT HAD COME ALONG IN A LONG TIME, SO I GOT OUT AND HANDED HIM THE STEERING WHEEL. I'D SAY IT WORKED OUT, WOULDN'T YOU?"

THE OWNER KNEW ALL TOO WELL

THE STRUGGLE TO SURVIVE ON SPONSOR SCRAPS AND SECONDHAND EQUIPMENT.

HE ALSO KNEW THAT ONLY A RARE TALENT COULD MAKE UP FOR A LACK OF FUNDING. BUT EVEN THE MOST PRECOCIOUS DRIVERS ARE QUICKLY FORGOTTEN ONCE THE SHORTAGE OF MEAL MONEY FORCES THEM TO PACK UP AND GO HOME.

"IF I HAD JUST DISAPPEARED WITHOUT A RIDE, NOBODY MIGHT HAVE EVER GIVEN ME ANOTHER SHOT," EARNHARDT TOLD *ESPN THE MAGAZINE* IN 1999.

"I MIGHT HAVE BEEN BACK ON THE SHORT TRACKS AND BACK WORKING IN A TEXTILE MILL SOME WHERE. HE SAVED MY BUTT. AND I NEVER FORGOT THAT."

Earnhardt and Childress parted ways for two years but quickly reunited for the 1984 campaign. Over two seasons, they picked up six wins, slowing their forward progress somewhat by either wrecking or detonating an engine on eleven different occasions. "Then came 1986," Earnhardt liked to say as his famous mustache parted into a grin, "and we had 'em right where we wanted 'em for about ten years."

THEY LIVED TOGETHER ON THE ROAD, WORKED TOGETHER AT THE TRACK,

AND ALONG THE WAY DID WHAT ALL FAMILIES DO—THEY ARGUED.

They argued about chassis setups, about pit strategies, about sponsorships and contracts. Fans purchased radio frequency scanners for no other reason than to listen to Dale and Richard bicker back and forth, lap after lap. No racer likes to be told what to do. Imagine, then, what happens when two racers find themselves butting heads while standing on the same tiny bandwidth.

No one in their path stood a chance.

Danny "Chocolate" Myers was the gas can man for the Flying Aces crew and front-row witness to each and every spat. "At first," he says, "they would get to yelling and we would all look at each other like, what is up with these guys? But after a while you realized that there was a method to the whole thing."

Like true kin, Dale and R.C. reached consensus when presented with a pressing decision. As with any great sports pairing, they knew when to yield to each other's expertise.

"From a crew chief standpoint, it would get a little unnerving," Larry McReynolds once admitted. "Richard knew when to push Dale's buttons to get him going in the right direction, and Dale knew how to get Richard mad so he could get what he wanted. And here the crew chief is in the middle of it. That's when you had to remind yourself that these guys had already won fifty or sixty races together. So you learned quick to just let them go and be glad they are on your team."

DURING THE WEEK,

THEY PROWLED MADISON AVENUE WITH THE SAME TRACKING SMARTS, SEARCHING FOR ANOTHER SUIT WILLING TO PAY FOR THE CHANCE TO SLAP HIS LOGO ON THE SIDE OF THE GREATEST SHOW IN RACING.

THE TENSION WAS TEMPOARY. THE STRENGTH OF THE FRIENDSHIP WAS UNMISTAKABLE AND EVERLASTING. DURING THE OFF-SEASON, THE TWO MEN DISAPPEARED INTO THE FORESTS OF MONTANA TO TRACK BIG GAME. CHILDRESS TOLD EARNHARDT THAT HE WOULD HAVE WON SEVENTY RACES HIMSELF IF GIVEN THE RIGHT EQUIPMENT. DALE REMINDED RICHARD THAT THE ONLY REASON HE HAD A MONTANA RANCH IN THE FIRST PLACE WAS BECAUSE HE HAD BEEN SMART ENOUGH TO HIRE AN EARNHARDT TO DRIVE HIS CARS.

TIME AND TIME AGAIN,

THE CORPORATE TITANS TRIED TO TALK EARNHARDT INTO STARTING HIS OWN WINSTON CUP TEAM. AND SO HE DID, RECRUITING THE LIKES OF PENZOIL, NAPA, AND ANHEUSER-BUSCH TO UNDERWRITE THE EXPANSION OF DALE EARNHARDT INCORPORATED. HE WENT LOOKING FOR DRIVERS AS WELL. HE ALREADY HAD A RIDE AND A LIFELONG DEBT TO REPAY.

Childress often wonders aloud about the ease with which Earnhardt could have left Richard Childress Racing to pilot his own car, but he always counters that thought with the memory of a pledge that Earnhardt made to him years ago. The pledge that said that as long as Dale Earnhardt was driving, he was going to drive for Richard Childress, because Childress had once taken a chance by placing his career—his entire future—in the hands of a driver no one else wanted.

THE RESULT

WAS A RUN OF SUCCESS THAT WILL LIKELY NEVER BE DUPLICATED IN THE INCREASINGLY COMPETITIVE WORLD OF NASCAR RACING. THESE DAYS, WHEN ALL OF THOSE LAPS, ALL OF THOSE ARGUMENTS, AND ALL OF THOSE LONG NIGHTS AT THE SHOP TEND TO RUN TOGETHER IN THE REPLAYS OF THE MIND, ONE ENDURING IMAGE STANDS OUT WITH CRYSTAL CLARITY.

It is the one of the two business associates, the two racers, the two friends. The smiling pair standing side-by-side in Victory Lane. Each with one arm draped around his partner and one arm wrapped around a gaudy gold cup. The money, the success, the sport-changing ideas all but forgotten in the wake of the ultimate payoff—that precious, fleeting moment of celebration. ***THE MOMENT WHEN 1 PLUS 1 EQUALS NOTHING LESS THAN 3.***

IT IS INDEED A RARE OCCURRENCE WHEN RIVAL RACERS BECOME BEST BUDS. RICHARD PETTY AND DAVID PEARSON GOT ALONG JUST FINE, THANK YOU, BUT THEY DIDN'T EXACTLY INVITE EACH OTHER OVER FOR DINNER AFTER THE CHECKERED FLAG WAS THROWN. CALE YARBOROUGH AND THE ALLISON BROTHERS LIKE TO TOUT THEIR MUTUAL LOVE, BUT THEIR STATED AFFECTION NEVER SEEMS TO WIPE AWAY THOSE IMAGES OF THE TRIO BEATING THE HELL OUT OF ONE ANOTHER ON NATIONAL TELEVISION AT THE 1979 DAYTONA 500.

NEIL BONNETT

RIVAL RACERS

THIS TIME-HONORED RELUCTANCE OF FAST MEN TO BECOME FAST FRIENDS IS WHAT MADE NEIL BONNETT AND DALE EARNHARDT SO SPECIAL. NEIL AND DALE, DALE AND NEIL. THEY WALKED ALIKE, TALKED ALIKE, AND FOR THE BETTER PART OF TWO DECADES WERE SELDOM SEEN APART.

"I'VE GOT TWO BROTHERS," EARNHARDT TOLD AN ESPN CAMERA CREW IN 1997. "I LOVE THOSE BOYS MORE THAN THEY KNOW. BUT MY RELATIONSHIP WITH NEIL WAS A TOTALLY DIFFERENT KIND OF LOVE. IT WAS THAT KIND OF LOVE WHERE YOU DON'T EVEN HAVE TO TALK. HE JUST KNEW WHAT I WAS THINKING, AND I KNEW WHAT HE WAS THINKING ALL THE TIME. WE NEVER HAD TO ASK EACH OTHER WHAT WE WERE DOING OR WHERE WE WERE GOING. WE JUST WENT AND DID."

BEFORE THEY WERE NEIL AND DALE, THEY WERE BONNETT AND EARNHARDT, TWO KIDS WITH IDENTICAL BLUE COLLARS, BUSHY MUSTACHES, AND THE DESIRE TO FIND THEIR NICHE IN A NASCAR WORLD RULED BY THE KING.

IN THE MID-1970S, THEY INTRODUCED THEMSELVES ON THE SHORT-TRACK BULL-RINGS OF THE SOUTH

Not with pressed palms and smiles, but with smacked-flat sheet metal and lone fingers raised high in the air. It was love at first slight.

"WE WERE FROM DIFFERENT PLACES, BUT THEY WERE STILL THE SAME," BONNETT EXPLAINED TO A GROUP OF DAYTONA BEAT WRITERS IN 1990. "HE WAS A NORTH CAROLINA LINT HEAD AND I HAD BEEN AN ALABAMA PIPE FITTER. WE WORKED ON OUR JOBS DURING THE DAY AND ON OUR CARS DURING THE NIGHT. WE APPRE- CIATED EACH OTHER RIGHT FROM THE START."

IN 1977, NEIL

WAS WINNING WINSTON CUP RACES AS AN ESTABLISHED MEMBER OF THE ALLISON BROTHERS' FAMED ALABAMA GANG. DALE WAS FIVE YEARS YOUNGER AND TWO YEARS BEHIND. BY THE SUMMER OF 1979, THEY WERE BOTH IN BIG-LEAGUE RIDES FULL-TIME, ALMOST IMMEDIATELY RUNNING DOOR-TO-DOOR. THEIR DRIVING STYLES WERE AS SIMILAR AS THEIR SWAGGERS. WIN FIRST, ASK FOR FORGIVENESS LATER. DURING THOSE SPLIT SECONDS WHEN THEY WERE AFFORDED A GLANCE OUT THE SIDE WINDOW, THEY FOUND THE SAME THOUGHT SPEEDING THROUGH THEIR MINDS . . .

AM I LOOKING INTO A MIRROR?

"If he was driving deeper into the corner than anyone else, I was probably doing the same," Earnhardt remembered. "Everybody else thought we were nuts, but once I realized that someone in the garage actually thought I was normal, I wanted to get to know that guy!"

During those lonely days when a rookie racer has to fight for a seat at the table, nothing calms the nerves like family. Without true blood kin on hand, Neil and Dale figured that the man most like himself would have to do.

"Earnhardt never got close to anybody," says Petty. "Especially in those first years when he showed up and started racing us. Number one, he wanted to seem tough. Number two, we were all too mad at him to get to know him. But with Bonnett it was different. Those two were separated at birth."

THE PAIR RACED AGAINST EACH OTHER 296 TIMES BETWEEN 1976 AND 1993, DALE FINISHING AHEAD OF NEIL 189 TIMES TO NEIL'S 107, ALTHOUGH NEIL SCOFFED AT HIS RIVAL'S OBSESSION WITH NUMBERS. ON OCCASION, THEY FINISHED A RACE BY CLIMBING OUT OF THEIR CARS AND SCREAMING AT EACH OTHER; MORE OFTEN THEY HUGGED. BUT THE TRUE ROOT OF THE FRIENDSHIP WAS NOT NURSED ON THE BLACKTOPS OF DARLINGTON OR DAYTONA. IT WAS FORGED IN THE DEER STANDS AND DUCK BLINDS SCATTERED ACROSS EASTERN ALABAMA AND THE NORTH CAROLINA PIEDMONT, IN THE KINDS OF MOMENTS THAT MEN LIKE TO SHARE OVER AND OVER AGAIN. WORDLESS REMEMBRANCES THAT ALWAYS END WITH A LAUGH AND A SHAKE OF THE HEAD.

NEIL BONNETT

WHEN THE TWO DECIDED TO BREAK IN A PAIR OF NEW **4X4 VEHICLES**, EARNHARDT PROMPTLY HAMMERED BONNETT'S RIDE. AS HE CLIMBED FROM THE TIRE-MARKED MESS, NEIL LOOKED UP AT HIS SMILING ALTER EGO.

"I DIDN'T WANT YOU TO GET INTO ALL THIS BRUSH AND HAVE TO SPEND ALL DAY WOR-RYING ABOUT IT GETTING SCRATCHED UP," DALE SAID.

AFTER **YEARS OF RIBBING** ABOUT HIS FOUL CABIN COOKING, BONNETT EARNED AN APOLOGY FROM HIS PAL AFTER A SUMPTUOUS FEAST OF PRIME RIB AND POTATOES. "WHEN DID YOU HAVE TIME TO LEARN TO COOK?" EARNHARDT SHOUTED TO THE MAN TOILING AWAY IN THE KITCHEN. "I'VE ALWAYS BEEN ABLE TO COOK, YOU JUST DIDN'T GIVE ME A CHANCE," CHEF BONNETT REPLIED. A SHORT TIME LATER, BONNETT'S SON DAVID WALKED INTO THE ROOM TO ASK HOW HIS MOM'S MEAL WENT OVER.

WHEN A PARTICULARLY IRRITABLE **DEER TRIED TO RUN HIS ANTLERS THROUGH BONNETT** DURING AN AFTERNOON OF SOLO FISHING ON THE EARNHARDT FARM, NEIL WENT TO THE TRUCK FOR HIS **GUN** AND **SHOT THE BUCK REPEATEDLY** UNTIL HE KNEW IT WAS GOOD AND DEAD. THIS SEEMED LIKE A LOGICAL SOLUTION UNTIL DALE EXPLAINED THAT THE OFFENDING CREATURE WAS HIS **DAUGHTER'S PET**.

"YOU WOULD GET TO THE TRACK EACH FRIDAY MORNING AND BREATHE A SIGH OF RELIEF WHEN THEY BOTH CAME WALKING INTO THE GARAGE," SAYS RICHARD CHILDRESS. "SOMEHOW THEY HAD SURVIVED ANOTHER WEEK WITHOUT KILLING EACH OTHER."

1990

EARNHARDT WAS WORKING ON HIS FOURTH NASCAR WINSTON CUP TITLE. BONNETT, THE VICTOR IN EIGHTEEN RACES, WAS LOOKING TO END A NEARLY TWO-YEAR WINLESS DROUGHT BEHIND THE WHEEL OF THE FAMED WOOD BROTHERS FORD WHEN A HARD CRASH OFF OF TURN 4 AT DARLINGTON ENDED HIS SEASON. DALE DROPPED THE HAMMER, KEEPING ONE EYE ON MARK MARTIN IN THE REARVIEW MIRROR AND ONE FINGER ON THE RADIO BUTTON, DEMANDING CONSTANT UPDATES FROM HIS PIT CREW ON THE CONDITION OF HIS FRIEND. AFTER EARNING HIS FIFTH WIN IN HIS LAST NINE RACES AT THE TRACK, HE HEADED STRAIGHT TO THE HOSPITAL AND LEARNED THAT BONNETT HAD SUFFERED SERIOUS HEAD INJURIES THAT LEFT HIM WITH AMNESIA.

The first memory Bonnett recalled wasn't from Victory Lane or from the births of his children. It was from a jack-jawing, deer-hunting trip to the woods with Earnhardt.

"I didn't like that feeling," Earnhardt said later. "Being helpless while he was just sitting . . . Looking into his eyes and wondering if he even knew who I was. When we got him through that, I knew I was never going to take our friendship for granted again."

Dale kept right on winning: that fourth title, which he dedicated to Neil, and championships five and six, recorded under the watchful eye of his buddy high up in the CBS Sports booth.

"I'm trying to stay impartial," Bonnett told play-by-play man Ken Squier during a commercial break in 1992. "But I'm doing a damn poor job of it."

ABOVE // NEIL BONNETT BEING HELPED FROM HIS CAR
AFTER A MULTI-CAR PILEUP IN THE 1982 DAYTONA 500.

WHEN BONNETT

GOT THE ITCH TO RACE,

Earnhardt offered his support. He put Neil to work as a test driver for Richard Childress Racing, letting him rack up thousands of miles on the track in the 3 car. Each visit to Victory Lane brought more praise, Dale crediting Neil with the legwork that allowed the GM Goodwrench team to grab the glory.

But testing just wasn't enough, as both drivers acknowledged in a hurry. Childress and Earnhardt soon had Bonnett back behind the wheel at his home track of Talladega, a race that ended with a frightening airborne crash into the front-stretch fence. Neil wanted more. He returned to the cockpit fourteen weeks later, helping Dale to clinch his sixth title.

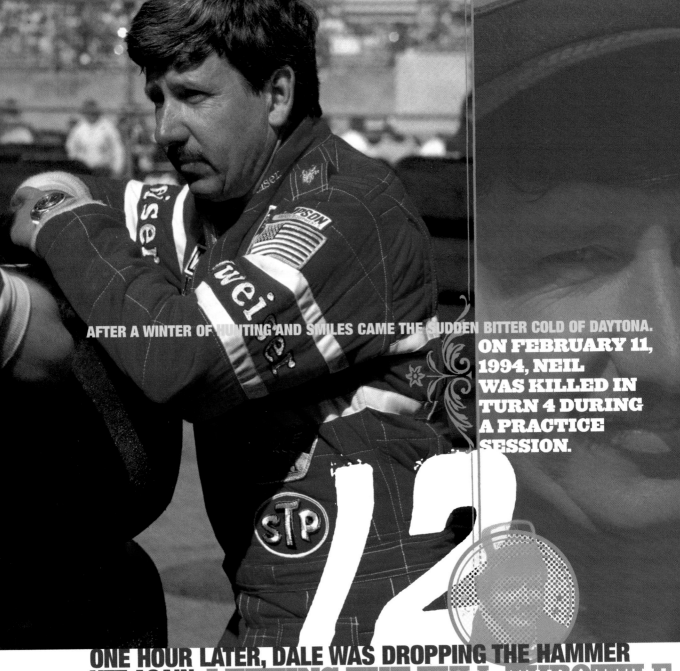

AFTER A WINTER OF HUNTING AND SMILES CAME THE SUDDEN BITTER COLD OF DAYTONA.

ON FEBRUARY 11, 1994, NEIL WAS KILLED IN TURN 4 DURING A PRACTICE SESSION.

ONE HOUR LATER, DALE WAS DROPPING THE HAMMER YET AGAIN, LETTING THE FULL-THROTTLE SONG OF HIS SMALL-BLOCK CHEVY DO HIS CRYING FOR HIM.

One week later, he was in Victory Lane with his friend's name painted brightly onto the trademark black of his car.

Ten months after that, he was celebrating title number seven when he finally let the tears flow over the loss of his friend.

"I MISS MY BUDDY,"

THE CHAMP ADMITTED. "I MISS HIM BEING HERE FOR THE GOOD TIMES, AND I MISS HIM GIVING ME HELL OVER THE BAD TIMES. I DO THE SAME THINGS I ALWAYS DID, BUT NONE OF IT FEELS THE SAME. I'M JUST GOING TO KEEP ON WINNING. THAT'S THE BEST WAY I KNOW TO PAY TRIBUTE. **BUT I DO MISS MY BUDDY.**"

CHAPTER

DAYTONA 500

ERES

Earnhardt

ACCORDING TO THE GUYS IN DALE'S GARAGE, TERESA WAS THE ONLY PERSON ON THE PLANET WHO COULD INTIMIDATE THE INTIMIDATOR.

// DALE AND HIS MOTHER, MARTHA, CELEBRATE HIS FIRST WINSTON CUP VICTORY AT BRISTOL IN 1979.

THE EARNHARDT WOMEN HAVE ALWAYS BEEN A STRONG-WILLED BUNCH. DALE'S MOTHER, MARTHA, SET THE STANDARD, BOLDLY STEPPING UP WHEN NECESSARY TO SUPPORT HER HUSBAND'S PASSION.

She raised five children on a shoestring budget, sacrificed her backyard to car parts, and when Ralph and his friends stumbled home from the track at 2 A.M., she was there in the kitchen to set out a meal for them. Family lore has it that she even raced his car in a powder puff derby, taking it for a spin—side over side. Dale's sister Kathy went one step better, grinding out a nine-race winning streak. And Dale's daughter Kelley drove late-model stock cars when she could find crewmen secure enough in their manhood to help her piece them together. Dale's wife, Teresa? Well, she quietly became the **MOST POWERFUL WOMAN** in NASCAR. According to the guys in Dale's garage, she was the only person on the planet who could intimidate The Intimidator.

THEY MET IN 1974 AT THE HICKORY MOTOR SPEEDWAY, THE ASPHALT OVAL THAT MADE TERESA'S UNCLE TOMMY HOUSTON A BUSCH SERIES LEGEND. HER FATHER, HAL HOUSTON—A DRIVER AS WELL—INTRODUCED THEM.

TERESA WAS SIXTEEN YEARS OLD. DALE WAS TWENTY-THREE.

They started dating in 1978, when Teresa was studying interior design at Piedmont Community College; she had raced through high school in three years.

Dale wasn't what you might call a great catch. He had two ex-wives, three kids, and limited prospects. He was scrambling to scratch out a living on the track. He had big dreams though, and Teresa understood them.

"I GREW UP AROUND RACING," SHE TOLD NBC'S KATIE COURIC IN 2003, "SO IT'S SECOND NATURE TO ME. IT'S JUST LIKE OTHER SPORTS; BULLRIDING, MOTORCYCLE RACING, BOXING . . . I DON'T UNDERSTAND WHY [PEOPLE] DO THOSE THINGS. BUT THEY KNOW WHAT THEY'RE DOING. IT'S A CHOICE."

As far as Dale was concerned, it was choice A, B, C, and D. He grew up with a one-track mind: everything beyond the track was secondary. Money? Marriage? Babies? No way. Nothing else could compete with the thrill of a Saturday night showdown.

TERESA UNDERSTOOD THIS. SHE NEVER ONCE TRIED TO RESIST IT.

She later admitted that she was attracted to Dale's energy and his confidence. "He was not too timid about doing whatever job needed to be done," she said. Dale in turn was smitten by her beauty and her intelligence. They shared a matching set of down-home country values.

Even so, it took Dale four years to ask her to marry him. Twice burned, he was reluctant to commit himself to another hasty decision. In July 1982, he tagged the rear bumper of Tim Richmond's Buick in the first turn at Pocono, slammed head-on into the wall, and landed upside down on the track. Dale limped off with a fractured kneecap. After wrecking again at Talladega the following week, he went into the hospital for repairs. While lying there in bed, he popped the question. He made it clear this was a package deal that included his daughter Kelley, son Dale Jr., and, of course, the world of stock car racing. Teresa accepted. They were married on November 14. Dale inscribed the date inside his wedding ring.

THE LIFE OF A NASCAR WIFE IS NEVER EASY.

THE OTHER HALF IS FOREVER ON THE ROAD, TOILING AWAY UNDER INSANELY COMPETITIVE CONDITIONS. SUCCESS IS MEASURED IN FRACTIONS OF A SECOND. MINOR MISTAKES INVITE TRAGEDY AND DEATH. TERESA EMBRACED THE BAD WITH THE GOOD. They started out in a small house near Charlotte, sleeping on a mattress on the floor. They draped bedsheets over the windows. "She was there when I didn't have anything," Dale explained, "and she stuck in there with me. She was there for the bad times . . . Shoot, I thought we were rich . . . I never wanted for anything. Teresa and I both came from a hard-luck background where we take what we have and make the best of it."

// FROM EARLY ON IN THEIR
MARRIAGE DALE AND TERESA
WERE A FORMIDABLE TEAM.

IN 1979 — HIS ROOKIE OF THE YEAR SEASON —

DALE BROUGHT HOME $30,000. *"I COULDN'T BELIEVE IT. JUST DRIVING A RACE CAR I MADE $30,000,"* HE SAID. FOR A MAN THRILLED TO BE EARNING A LIVING BEHIND THE WHEEL, THAT WAS A TRUCKLOAD OF MONEY. BUT IT WAS A PITTANCE COMPARED WITH WHAT WAS TO COME.

TERESA

TERESA

IN PUBLIC, TERESA IS QUIET AND RESERVED.

Put her in a corporate boardroom, however, and she is every bit the intimidator herself. When Dale Earnhardt Inc. was founded in 1980, it was little more than a name. The entire operation fit snugly into a three-bay garage. Three years later, Teresa took charge of the company. Her assets included a desk, a phone, and a typewriter. But long before the dawn of sports marketing, she recognized the value of her husband's image and she moved quickly to protect it with trademarks. Armed with nothing more than a real estate license, she combed through the minutiae in every contract Dale signed, demanding translation when the legal language confused her and taking note of the terms she particularly liked so she could request them again. She all but created The Man in Black, negotiating Dale's schedule, handpicking his merchandise, and approving every photograph of him that graced a racing program. She did this without fanfare.

Today, Dale Earnhardt Inc. is housed in a glistening, 200,000-square-foot complex known far and wide as Garage Mahal. One hundred fifty employees staff the offices, race shop, museum, and souvenir store. Dale and Teresa eventually owned several homes, a 350-acre chicken farm, an auto dealership, three Winston Cup cars, four airplanes, a helicopter, a 76-foot yacht named *Sunday Money,* a seat on the New York Stock Exchange, and a piece of minor league baseball's Kannapolis Intimidators. Their total worth was valued at more than $100 million. As Dale Jr. likes to point out, "Dad always said that before he met Teresa he owed the bank money. And after they got married the bank owed him money."

Much like Martha Earnhardt, Teresa made it possible for her husband to focus on his career. She handled all of the ancillary stuff, dictating the terms on everything from his sponsorship deals to his diet. A family friend remembers receiving a phone call one morning from Teresa's mischievous husband, who summoned him to the garage—immediately.

"What's going on?" the friend asked.

"TERESA'S OUT OF TOWN!" DALE CHIRPED. "WE'RE HAVING STEAK AND POTATOES FOR LUNCH!"

ABOVE // DALE EARNHARDT SWEPT UP THE COMPETITION—AND THE MILLION DOLLAR BONUS—BY WINNING THE '99 WINSTON 500 AT TALLADEGA.

BEYOND THE TALES OF CONFLICT AND MONEY, HOWEVER, IT'S HARD TO PIN TERESA DOWN. SHE FANCIES HER PRIVACY AND FRIENDS ARE LOATH TO SHARE THE DETAILS OF HER LIFE. BUT THIS MUCH IS CERTAIN: TERESA MADE DALE A HAPPY MAN. BEFORE THEY MET, HE HAD LITTLE CONFIDENCE IN HIS VALUE OUTSIDE OF THE DRIVER'S SEAT OF A RACE CAR. HE SAW HIMSELF AS SOMETHING OF AN INTROVERT, A SMALL-TOWN BOY LIMITED BY HIS LACK OF EDUCATION. HE HAD GIVEN UP PARENTAL RIGHTS TO HIS FIRSTBORN SON BECAUSE HE COULDN'T MEET HIS CHILD SUPPORT PAYMENTS, AND HE WAS AN ABSENTEE FATHER TO HIS NEXT TWO CHILDREN BECAUSE OF THE CRAZY DEMANDS OF HIS JOB. HE WAS UNCOMFORTABLE WITH SMALL TALK, OFTEN PRICKLY WITH THE MEDIA. IT WAS TERESA WHO CHANGED ALL THAT. IT WAS TERESA WHO MOLDED HIM INTO A LEG:

ABOVE // DALE AND TERESA JOYFULLY CELEBRATE HIS LONG-AWAITED VICTORY IN THE 1998 DAYTONA 500.

With her unwavering support, she gave Dale the courage to reach for his dreams. She anticipated his every need, offering him counsel when he wanted it and unlimited encouragement. She created a safe haven far from the track, a sprawling retreat where he could lose himself in odd chores and repair his relationships with his children. When sixteen-year-old Kerry showed up unannounced one day, after living with his mom for eleven years, Teresa welcomed the boy into their home and pressed Dale into opening his heart to him. She tended to Kelley and Dale Jr. whenever they needed school clothes or checkups. And she presented Dale with the opportunity to correct his mistakes by giving him a baby daughter in December 1988. With Taylor Nicole, Dale was hands-on from the start. He led her from the nursery to the garage to the racetrack.

PEOPLE WHO WATCHED HER GROW UP JOKE THAT HER FIRST WORD WAS "CARBURETOR."

MAYBE IT WAS FORTUNATE THAT TERESA MET DALE WHEN HE WAS A DIRT-TRACK DEMON INSTEAD OF YEARS LATER, WHEN HE WAS A GENUINE SUPERSTAR. NO ONE COULD EVER QUESTION HER LOVE FOR THE MAN. JUST THE SAME, IT'S HARD TO IMAGINE THINGS TURNING OUT ANY DIFFERENTLY.

Teresa arrived on the scene secure about herself, confident enough in her abilities to resist competing with the public for Dale's attention. In their nineteen years of marriage, she rarely gave interviews. She seemed almost to shun the spotlight, except for those fleeting Sunday afternoons when she stood behind her husband in Victory Lane, quietly urging him to reveal his true self to the fans. It took years, but gradually Dale grew more at ease in the presence of strangers. When at last he discovered how much they admired him, he glowed with good will. In the days before that final run at Daytona, before he hugged his son and walked hand-in-hand down pit road with Taylor and Teresa, he told his old pal Darrell Waltrip that he was the luckiest man in the world. "I've had a great career," Dale said. "Got a great wife, a great family. I'm a guy who has it all."

OPPOSITE BOTTOM // BEFORE CELEBRATING HIS VICTORY AT DAYTONA (LEFT), DALE AND TERESA ATTENDED NASCAR'S FIFTIETH ANNIVERSARY CELEBRATION, AT WHICH DALE WAS HONORED AS ONE OF THE FIFTY GREATEST DRIVERS.

WITHOUT TERESA, HE HAD NEXT TO NOTHING.

THE KIDS

106 THE KIDS

DALE EARNHARDT DID NOT SPEND MUCH TIME LOOKING IN THE REARVIEW MIRROR. HE DIDN'T OFTEN SPEAK OF REGRETS, BUT HE HAD A FEW. IN THE EARLY DAYS OF HIS CAREER, HE RACED TOWARD THE FUTURE WITH SUCH SINGLE-MINDED DETERMINATION THAT HE LEFT BEHIND SOME IMPORTANT PIECES OF HIS LIFE. AMONG THE CASUALTIES OF HIS QUEST FOR SUCCESS WERE HIS RELATIONSHIPS WITH HIS FIRST THREE CHILDREN. HIS OLDEST SON, KERRY, WAS ADOPTED BY HIS STEPFATHER AT AN EARLY AGE BECAUSE DALE COULDN'T AFFORD TO MEET HIS CHILD SUPPORT PAYMENTS. DAUGHTER KELLEY AND SON DALE JR. WERE LEFT IN THE CARE OF TERESA, THEIR STEPMOTHER, WHILE THEIR DAD STORMED AHEAD IN SEARCH OF HIS DREAMS.

// TERESA WAS ALWAYS THERE FOR DALE'S CHILDREN, KELLEY (LEFT) AND DALE JR.

DALE WAS EIGHTEEN YEARS OLD, MARRIED LESS THAN A YEAR, WHEN KERRY WAS BORN. SCRAMBLING TO MAKE ENDS MEET, THE YOUNG DRIVER COBBLED TOGETHER A SERIES OF ODD JOBS: PUMPING GAS AT THE SUNOCO STATION, SWINGING A WRENCH WITH THE MAINTENANCE CREW AT CANNON MILLS, CHANGING TIRES AT PUNCH'S WHEEL ALIGNMENT SERVICE, WELDING AT GREAT DANE TRAILERS IN CHARLOTTE—WHATEVER MEANS HE COULD FIND TO BRING HOME A PAYCHECK. AT NIGHT, HE WORKED ON HIS RACE CAR. HIS 24/7 SCHEDULE DIDN'T LEAVE MUCH ROOM FOR BEDTIME STORIES. HIS MARRIAGE TO LATANE BROWN CRUMBLED AS A RESULT.

AT AGE TWENTY, NONE THE WISER, DALE WED BRENDA GEE, THE DAUGHTER OF A RENOWNED LOCAL GARAGE OWNER. WITHIN THREE YEARS, HE HAD TWO NEW MOUTHS TO FEED: KELLEY AND DALE JR. LIFE WAS ONE LONG STRUGGLE. "WE PROBABLY SHOULD HAVE BEEN ON WELFARE," DALE SAID. "WE DIDN'T HAVE MONEY TO BUY GROCERIES." THE FAMILY MOVED AROUND A LOT, SETTLING INTO TINY APARTMENTS OR TRAILER HOMES. DALE BORROWED MONEY FOR CAR PARTS, HOPING TO WIN IT BACK AT THE TRACK. BUT RACING IS A RISKY BUSINESS. THINGS DON'T ALWAYS GO AS PLANNED. HE SOON FOUND HIMSELF $11,000 IN THE HOLE.

BRENDA HELD ON TIGHT FOR FIVE LONG YEARS BEFORE SHE, TOO, CALLED IT QUITS. IN 1980, HER EX-HUSBAND WAS RACING TOWARDS HIS FIRST WINSTON CUP CHAMPIONSHIP WHEN THE SHODDY WIRING IN HER HOME SET THE KITCHEN ABLAZE. EVERYONE SURVIVED, BUT THE HOUSE WAS GUTTED. KELLEY AND JUNIOR ESCAPED TO DALE'S PLACE. KELLEY WAS EIGHT. JUNIOR WAS SIX. THEIR FATHER HAD NO TIME FOR DANCE RECITALS OR LITTLE LEAGUE. "TERESA RAISED THEM," HE SAID FLATLY. "I DIDN'T DO MUCH."

HAD NO TROUBLE, IT SEEMS, BONDING WITH THE CHILDREN OF OTHER MEN. HE ALWAYS FOUND TIME FOR THE YOUNG FANS AT THE TRACK, THE TERMINALLY ILL BOYS AND GIRLS OF THE MAKE-A-WISH FOUNDATION. WITH HIS OWN KIDS, HOWEVER, HE WAS FAR LESS ACCESSIBLE. FOR ALTHOUGH HE COULD DIVINE THE INTRICATE WORKINGS OF THE COSMOS FROM THE DRIVER'S SEAT OF A RACE CAR, HE COULD NOT READILY GRASP THE COMPLEXITIES OF FATHERHOOD.

HE WAS BEFUDDLED BY THE WAYS

// DALE AND HIS
DAUGHTER TAYLOR
NICOLE AT THE
ATLANTA 500 IN 1994.

OF YOUTH,

THE VIDEO GAMES, THE COMPUTERS, THE MUSIC. HE COULD NOT FATHOM WHY HIS CHILDREN DID NOT RISE FROM BED TO GREET THE DAY AT DAWN.

THE EARNHARDT CHILDREN WERE EQUALLY MYSTIFIED BY THEIR FATHER.

HE WAS GRUFF AND UNPREDICTABLE, NOT MUCH GOOD AT SMALL TALK AND DEMANDING AS A ROLE MODEL. ONCE HE SLICED HIS HAND TO THE BONE WHILE CUTTING DOWN A TREE IN THE BACKYARD WITH A CHAINSAW. HE DIDN'T EVEN PAUSE TO LOOK AT IT. "HE HAD SUCH HIGH STANDARDS," DALE JR. EXPLAINED. "HE HAD SUCH AUTHORITY, INTEGRITY, AND GRIT, THAT YOU STARTED ON A CERTAIN RUNG AND HAD TO EARN HIS RESPECT TO MOVE UP. I DEFINITELY HAD TO WORK MY WAY UP THE RANKS. IT TOOK A WHILE FOR US TO GET TO KNOW EACH OTHER."

// DALE'S SONS, DALE JR. AND KERRY, BOTH FOLLOWED IN THEIR FATHER'S TRACKS.

AT AGE ELEVEN,

JUNIOR STUMBLED ON A WAY TO SNARE HIS FATHER'S ATTENTION—IN THE COCKPIT OF A GO-KART. "HE CAME OFF A TURN AND HIS WHEEL GOT CLIPPED AND HE WENT STRAIGHT UP INTO THE AIR, TUMBLING HEAD OVER HEELS," HIS FATHER PROUDLY RECALLED. "WHEN HE STOPPED HIS LITTLE HANDS WENT UP AND HE STARTED WAVING. BY THE TIME HE STOPPED I'D RUN ACROSS THE TRACK AND WAS STANDING NEXT TO HIM. HE SAID, 'WHERE'S MY GO-KART?' THAT WAS THE ONLY THING HE WAS CONCERNED ABOUT. IT WAS PRETTY AWESOME."

KERRY MADE HIS MOVE AT AGE SIXTEEN, WALKING BACK INTO HIS FATHER'S LIFE UNANNOUNCED. IT WAS A WAKE-UP CALL OF SORTS. THE MAN IN BLACK WANTED TO MAKE AMENDS FOR ALL THE LOST YEARS, SO HE TRIED HIS BEST TO REACH OUT, EVEN THOUGH HE WASN'T SURE HOW TO PROCEED.

He wasn't much good with words. Kelley was away at college in Wilmington some years later when her father decided that it would be nice to have her closer to home. He sent flowers. "I kept the card," she recalled. "It said, 'It's been so long I have almost forgotten what you look like.'"

When Junior was sixteen, he dispensed with the celebrated go-kart. He took $200 from the sale, rushed off to the junkyard, and returned with a 1978 Monte Carlo, which he set about restoring with Kerry in the garage. Dale watched from the wings. Every now and then, he offered a bit of advice. Then he got some grease on his hands, fretting over the safety devices. (He was the one who pushed Junior to retire from go-kart racing after one year. "It's not safe," he said.) When the car was complete, the boys let her rip on the nearby racetracks, alternating weekends behind the wheel.

DULY IMPRESSED, DALE ORDERED UP TWO SPORTSMAN SERIES CARS FOR HIS SONS. WHEN KELLEY PROTESTED, HE MADE IT THREE. FOR TWO SEASONS, THE THREE SIBLINGS FLEW THE RED CLAY OVALS OF NORTH CAROLINA. ONCE THEY EVEN COMPETED AGAINST EACH OTHER—FOR PRECISELY ONE LAP. KERRY AND KELLEY WERE SWEPT FROM THE FIELD IN A CRASH.

KERRY INHERITED HIS FATHER'S FULL-THROTTLE FEARLESSNESS. JUNIOR WAS MORE RESERVED. "HE'S A THINKING DRIVER, A LITTLE CALMER THAN HIS DAD," CREW CHIEF TONY EURY SR. TOLD *ESPN THE MAGAZINE.* "WHEN HIS DAD STARTED OUT, HE WAS HIS OWN WORST ENEMY." JUNIOR'S CEREBRAL DRIVING STYLE ACTUALLY MIRRORED THAT OF HIS GRANDFATHER RALPH, THE ORIGINAL NUMBER 8. KELLEY? WELL, SHE RETIRED EARLY BECAUSE SHE COULD NOT ROUND UP ENOUGH OPEN-MINDED CREWMEN TO KEEP HER CAR RUNNING. HER YOUNGER BROTHER SAYS SHE SHOWED THE MOST PROMISE OF THE BUNCH.

Kerry married young, fathered two children, and left the track in search of a stable job. Kelley earned a business degree from the University of North Carolina at Charlotte. Junior was left on his own to shoulder the Earnhardt name. It was no easy task for a man of his slight build. His grade-school pals were not awed by the family patriarch's brash skills. They preferred to spar with their classmate over senior's reckless driving. Years later, in his first season in the late-model series, Junior was still being tested by his peers. He accepted the bumping and scraping as part of the initiation. But the moment he decided enough was enough, he ran his tormentor off the track—straight through a steel gate. Another fool took his whacks and Junior stopped him dead in his shoes.

"LET'S SOLVE THIS RIGHT NOW," HE SAID. "LET'S PUT OUR CARS ON THE TRACK. YOU GO THAT WAY, I'LL GO THIS WAY, AND WE'LL RUN HEAD-ON IN THE BACKSTRETCH." "YOU'RE CRAZY," THE DRIVER RESPONDED. JUNIOR SMILED, "THAT'S RIGHT."

AS IT TURNS OUT, HE INHERITED QUITE A BIT FROM THE OLD MAN: AN UNCOMMONLY LOW PULSE RATE, AN AVERSION TO CLASSWORK (ALTHOUGH HIS STORY CONCLUDES WITH A DIPLOMA), AND A HEAPING HELPING OF SCRAP. FOUR YEARS INTO HIS CAREER, JUNIOR SHIFTED INTO HIS FATHER'S BUSCH SERIES CAR AND STEERED IT TO BACK-TO-BACK CHAMPIONSHIPS. AS THE NEW MILLENNIUM APPROACHED, ANOTHER EARNHARDT VS. EARNHARDT SHOWDOWN WAS IN THE MAKING. THIS TIME, THE STAKES WERE HUGE. "JUNIOR?" DALE ANNOUNCED WITH BRAVADO. "HE'S JUST ANOTHER DRIVER. ON THE TRACK HE'S JUST ANOTHER COMPETITOR." BEFORE THE START OF AN IROC RACE IN 1999, THE INTIMIDATOR GAVE THE KID'S REAR BUMPER A FEW LOVE TAPS. LATER, HE EXPRESSED HIMSELF MORE EMPHATICALLY. THE TWO WERE RACING TWIN PONTIACS SIDE-BY-SIDE TOWARD THE CHECKERED FLAG IN MICHIGAN WHEN JUNIOR FOUND HIMSELF SPINNING OFF THE TRACK.

"HE RAN INTO ME," DALE INSISTED. ➤ "HE CREAMED ME," JUNIOR REPLIED.

DEEP IN HIS HEART, DALE EARNHARDT WAS THRILLED TO KNOW THAT HIS SON WANTED TO FOLLOW IN HIS TIRE TRACKS. FOR A LONG TIME, HE HAD NOT SEEN IT COMING. "HE NEVER SEEMED TO HAVE THE INTEREST," SENIOR SAID. JUNIOR INSISTS THAT THIS WAS SIMPLY A FAILURE TO COMMUNICATE. "I ALWAYS WANTED TO BE A DRIVER," HE SAYS. "BUT THERE WAS ALWAYS THIS IDEA THAT YOU HAD TO SWEEP THE FLOOR FOR A YEAR BEFORE YOU EVER GOT A CHANCE TO TOUCH A WRENCH. I DIDN'T WANT TO SWEEP THE FLOOR." MAYBE IT WAS NEGOTIATED AND MAYBE IT WAS PREORDAINED, THE PRIMORDIAL TUG OF THE FAMILY GENES, BUT THEY EVENTUALLY HIT ON A COMMON LANGUAGE. IT WAS SPELLED OUT ON THE RACETRACK. AFTER ESCAPING A MASSIVE PILEUP ON LAP 176 AT DAYTONA IN 2001, DALE SR. PULLED UP ALONGSIDE HIS SON AND GAVE HIM A PROUD THUMBS-UP. AS THE TWO MEN HURTLED TOWARD THE FINISH, SENIOR HELD FIRM TO THIRD PLACE, SHIELDING THE TWO CARS IN FRONT OF HIM FROM THE PACK. THE FIRST WAS DRIVEN BY MICHAEL WALTRIP. THE SECOND WAS PILOTED BY HIS SON.

"FIND YOUR OWN WAY HOME."

"THIS WAS AN ACT OF SELF LESS NESS…"

If you were watching closely one year earlier, you might have noticed the change. The Intimidator always hated to lose. Once upon a time, he would have bolted from the track in frustration seconds after a near miss. At Richmond in 2000, however, he learned the joy of soaking in the scenery. Junior had just recorded his second Winston Cup win in his sixteenth Winston Cup start. After easing to a halt, Dale saddled up to his side, pulling him close and whispering into his ear.

"CONGRATULATIONS SON, I LOVE YOU, FIND YOUR OWN WAY HOME."

CHAPTER

1 2 3 4 5 6 7 8 9

DAY

PEOPLE ALWAYS WANTED TO TAKE DALE EARNHARDT BACK IN TIME, TO THE ALAMO OR THE O.K. CORRAL, SOME FRONTIER OUTPOST WHERE HE WOULD GUN DOWN EVERYONE IN HIS PATH. AND WHY NOT? HE LOOKED THE PART, WITH THOSE STEELY BLUE EYES, THE BRUSHY MUSTACHE, AND THE SUN-BAKED LEATHER SKIN.

"I always said he looked like the last Confederate soldier," says Humpy Wheeler. "He looked like one of those guys in the old silver photos from Gettysburg or Manassas. Like he would have been much more comfortable out in the wilderness somewhere looking for a bad guy to shoot."

In 1990, ESPN convinced The Man in Black to don cowboy duds for a commercial filmed in the red rock desert of Arizona. When he came walking through the dust to meet rival Mark Martin in a *High Noon* showdown, the TV crew fell silent. "Damn," remarked a cameraman. "He looks like he's done this before."

He had. Every February of his adult life. With an itchy trigger finger twitching above his holster, he returned each winter to stare down his nemesis, the Daytona 500. And each winter for nearly two decades, Daytona won the duel.

"IT WAS UNBELIEVABLE," RACER-TURNED-ANALYST BENNY PARSONS SAYS. "IF YOU HAD WRITTEN THE STORY OF DALE AND THE DAYTONA 500 AND TAKEN IT TO HOLLYWOOD, THEY WOULD HAVE LAUGHED YOU OUT OF TOWN AND SAID, 'GET OUTTA HERE! NO ONE IS GOING TO BUY INTO THIS STORY. NO ONE HAS THIS MUCH BAD LUCK!'"

// DALE WITH LEGENDARY DRIVER CALE YARBOROUGH, FOUR-TIME WINNER OF THE DAYTONA 500.

BETWEEN 1979 & 1997

EARNHARDT TOOK THE GREEN FLAG IN THE GREAT AMERICAN RACE NINETEEN TIMES, ALMOST ALWAYS AS THE HEAVY FAVORITE. NINETEEN TIMES HE CAME UP EMPTY. WITH EACH LOSS, THERE SEEMED TO BE ONE MORE CAMERA AND ONE MORE REPORTER AT THE FINISH WAITING TO ASK HIM THE SAME QUESTIONS:

"WHAT HAPPENED? ARE YOU DISAPPOINTED? ARE YOU EVER GOING TO WIN THE BIG ONE?"

EVENTUALLY, THE MOB SWELLED INTO AN ARMY. TO ADDRESS THEM ALL, EARNHARDT HAD TO CLIMB ON TOP OF A TOOLBOX. HE SMILED A LITTLE BIGGER AND SHRUGGED HIS SHOULDERS A LITTLE HIGHER EACH YEAR, BUT NO ONE WAS BUYING THE ACT. HE WAS HURTING INSIDE.

IN 1986

HE WAS IN PERFECT POSITION TO SLINGSHOT PAST GEOFF BODINE FOR THE WIN WHEN HIS GAS TANK RAN DRY WITH THREE LAPS TO GO.

IN 1990

HE ENTERED TURN 3 ON THE FINAL LAP WITH THE LEAD. IN THE BLINK OF AN EYE, HIS RIGHT REAR TIRE RUPTURED, CRIPPLING HIS CHEVY AND HANDING THE WIN TO DERRIKE COPE.

IN 1993 & 1996

EARNHARDT SUCCUMBED TO CLOSING LAP PASSES BY DALE JARRETT. IN 1995, HE MADE A MAD DASH FROM THIRTEENTH TO SECOND IN THIRTEEN LAPS, ONLY TO FALL A CAR SHORT TO STERLING MARLIN. IN 1997, CAR NUMBER 3 ROLLED SIDE OVER SIDE EXITING TURN 2. "I'VE STILL NEVER WON THE DAYTONA 500," EARNHARDT ANNOUNCED TO THE SEA OF SCRIBES, "AND I AIN'T GOING TO DISNEY WORLD EITHER!"

During those first nineteen trips, he led the way for at least one lap in all but two races. He finished inside the top ten fourteen times, four as the runner-up. The saga of his losing streak was so gripping it overshadowed the multiple wins of Jarrett and Marlin.

ULTIMATELY, IT DID NOT MATTER WHERE EARNHARDT PLACED: FROM SECOND TO THIRTY-FIRST, HIS DISAPPO WAS THE STO

"DAD WOULD COME DOWN HERE AND JUST WIN EVERYTHING," DALE EARNHARDT JR. REMEMBERED AFTER CLAIMING HIS DAYTONA 500 VICTORY IN 2004 ON HIS FIFTH TRY. "HE WOULD WIN THE BUSCH CLASH, THE POLE FOR THE 500, A TWIN 125 QUALIFYING RACE, THE IROC RACE, THE BUSCH SERIES RACE ON SATURDAY, AND THEN SOMETHING WOULD ALWAYS HAPPEN ON SUNDAY. ALWAYS."

THE MAN IN BLACK FORCED THE OLD SPEEDWAY TO BLINK THIRTY-FOUR TIMES IN HIS CAREER. THIRTY-TWO OF THOSE VICTORIES WERE LOGGED DURING FEBRUARY'S SPEEDWEEKS—A RECORD OF DOMINATION THAT MADE HIS STRUGGLES IN THE 500 ALL THE MORE BAFFLING AND THE EVENTS OF FEBRUARY 15, 1998 SO MUCH MORE SPECIAL . . .

NTMENT

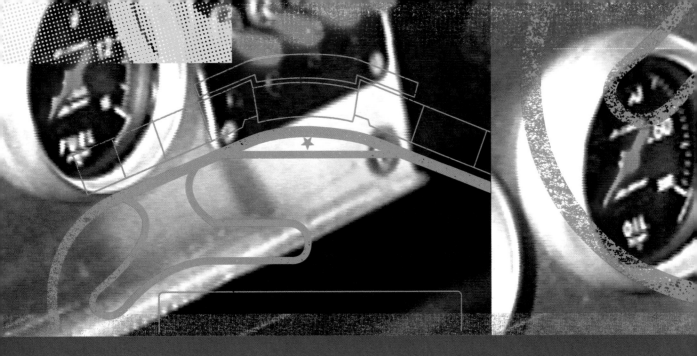

BY INTIMIDATOR STANDARDS, THAT TRIP TO DAYTONA WAS A QUIET WALK ON THE BEACH. EARNHARDT HAD WON A TWIN 125 QUALIFIER ON THURSDAY—HIS NINTH IN A ROW. AT A RECEPTION HONORING THE FIFTY GREATEST DRIVERS IN NASCAR HISTORY, HE SWAPPED STORIES WITH SEVEN-TIME DAYTONA 500 WINNER RICHARD PETTY, FOUR-TIME WINNER CALE YARBOROUGH, AND NEARLY EVERY OTHER LIVING WINNER OF HIS SPORT'S BIGGEST RACE. WHEN ASKED ABOUT HAVING TO DEFEND HIS OH-FOR-LIFE RECORD IN THE FACE OF ENDLESS RIBBING FROM BUDDY BAKER AND DARRELL WALTRIP, WHO HAD SNAPPED LENGTHY DROUGHTS OF THEIR OWN, EARNHARDT SAID, "IT JUST MAKES ME WANT TO GO OUT THERE AND DOMINATE ON SUNDAY. THEN WE'LL HAVE TO GET ALL THESE GUYS BACK TOGETHER AGAIN NEXT YEAR SO I CAN BRING MY TROPHY WITH ME AND POLISH IT UP IN FRONT OF THEM."

A GAME OF INCHES

1 INCH   2 INCHES   3 INCHES   4 INCHES   5 INCHES   6 IN

LUCKY PENNY

HE STARTED FOURTH ON AN OVERCAST AFTERNOON WITH A LUCKY PENNY GLUED TO THE INSTRUMENT PANEL AND A SURPRISE STOWED AWAY IN A SECRET LOCATION—A DINGY LITTLE STUFFED ANIMAL THAT LOOKED LIKE IT HAD BEEN DRAGGED ALL THE WAY DOWN I-95 FROM KANNAPOLIS TO DAYTONA. EARNHARDT WOULD PULL IT OUT ONLY IF THE TIME WAS RIGHT.

THOUGH THE STRING OF CLOSE LOSSES AT DAYTONA DOGGED DALE EARNHARDT, A COLD TRUTH OF MOTOR RACING IS THAT, WIN OR LOSE, IT'S A GAME OF INCHES. AT DARLINGTON IN 1982, HE BEAT CALE YARBOROUGH BY LESS THAN A CAR LENGTH. IN 1984, HE FINISHED JUST A FEW FEET BEHIND BENNY PARSONS IN THE COCA COLA 500, AND A PHOTO WAS NEEDED TO DETERMINE THAT HE'D EDGED TERRY LABONTE AND BUDDY BAKER IN THE TALLADEGA 500. AND IN PROBABLY THE CLOSEST FINISH OF HIS CAREER, EARNHARDT BEAT BOBBY LABONTE BY INCHES AFTER 325 LAPS IN THE 2000 CRACKER BARREL OLD COUNTRY STORE 500.

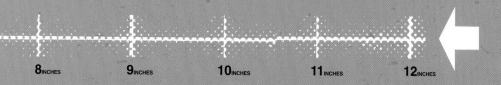

HES   8INCHES   9INCHES   10INCHES   11INCHES   12INCHES

ONE BY ONE, THE CHALLENGERS CAME TO THE REAR BUMPER OF THE NUMBER 3 CAR. GORDON, MARLIN, BOBBY LABONTE, RUSTY WALLACE, JEREMY MAYFIELD, AND TEAMMATE MIKE SKINNER. SKINNER, WITH WHOM EARNHARDT ENJOYED A TENSE RELATIONSHIP AT BEST, GAVE HIS CHILDRESS RACING MENTOR THE PUSH HE NEEDED TO BLAST INTO THE LEAD WITH TWENTY-THREE LAPS TO GO. FOR THE NEXT TEN MINUTES, THE 175,000 PEOPLE IN THE STANDS HELD THEIR COLLECTIVE BREATH.

WHAT WOULD IT BE THIS TIME?

WOULD LABONTE OR MAYFIELD SNEAK BY HIM FOR A FIRST 500 WIN? WOULD A STRAY FIFTY-CENT LUG NUT SLASH A TIRE? WOULD A DAMN METEOR SLAM INTO THE BACKSTRETCH? SOMETHING, *ANYTHING*, WAS BOUND TO HAPPEN, RIGHT?

WOULD A STRAY FIFTY-CENT LUGNUT SLASH ANOTHER TIRE?

FOR THE
NEXT 10
MINUTES
175,000
PEOPLE
IN THE STANDS
HELD THEIR
COLLECTIVE
BREATH.

THEN, AS IF THE CREATOR HIMSELF COULD NO LONGER STOMACH THE TENSION, A REAR-PACK WRECK BROUGHT OUT THE CAUTION FLAG WITH ONE LAP TO GO. JUST LIKE THAT, DALE'S TROUBLES WERE OVER. HE HAD WON THE DAYTONA 500 IN HIS TWENTIETH TRY.

He didn't waste time in Victory Lane waxing philosophical about all the near-misses. He didn't cry, quote Scripture, or bother to say, "I told you so." What he did do was pull out that pitiful little toy and throw it squarely at the media, most of whom were failing to document the moment and just standing there admiring the man.

"THERE YOU GO!" HE SHOUTED. "I'VE GOT THAT DAMN MONKEY OFF MY BACK!"

TWENTY-ONE DAYS EARLIER, JOHN ELWAY OF THE DENVER BRONCOS HAD WON HIS FIRST SUPER BOWL. EARNHARDT WELCOMED THE NEWS, COMMENDING THE QUARTERBACK ON HIS FIFTEEN YEARS OF FAITHFUL PURSUIT. "IF ELWAY CAN WIN A SUPER BOWL, THEN I CAN WIN THE DAYTONA 500," HE SAID BEFORE THE START OF THE RACE. GREAT ATHLETES WHO HAD BEEN TESTED BY THEIR NEMESES WAS A FAVORITE TOPIC. IN THE PAST, EARNHARDT HAD MENTIONED THE BOSTON RED SOX AND THE CHICAGO CUBS, THE THOROUGHBREDS THAT CAME UP SHORT IN THE TRIPLE CROWN, IVAN LENDL AND HIS FAILURE TO WIN AT WIMBLEDON. "I KNOW WHAT IT'S LIKE TO WONDER IF IT IS EVER GOING TO HAPPEN," HE SAID. "I ALWAYS FIGURED I'D BEAT HIS TAIL, BUT I DIDN'T KNOW WHEN."

// DALE EARNHARDT TAKES THE CHECKERED FLAG IN THE 1998 DAYTONA 500. FINALLY!

AFTER YEARS OF MATCHING WITS WITH THE DAYTONA INTERNATIONAL SPEEDWAY, EARNHARDT HAD COME TO THINK OF THE MASSIVE, 2.5-MILE OVAL AS A LIVING, BREATHING RIVAL. HE TALKED ABOUT ITS ATTITUDE AND ITS MOOD SWINGS. HE SPOKE OF THE DANGER OF ANGERING IT. IN THE FORTY-TWO YEARS SINCE THE TRACK HAD OPENED, NO LESS THAN TWENTY-SIX DRIVERS HAD DIED THERE.

In his maiden voyage on Daytona's asphalt, way back in July 1978, Earnhardt had rolled to a shocking seventh-place finish in an underfunded ride. The winner, David Pearson, beat him by three laps. Ralph Earnhardt had been just as impressive in his debut seventeen years earlier, finishing tenth, also behind Pearson. Dale had visited the track with his father several times in the early sixties. He never forgot what it felt like to emerge from the Turn 4 tunnel and take in the overwhelming size of the place.

It was a desire to return to that track that had him working through the night on his race cars as a teenager, that compelled him to walk through the Cup garage with his hat in his hand years later searching for a ride. The tremendous strain of his never-ending quest was magnified in 1994 by the trauma of losing Neil Bonnett in that Turn 4 practice crash. When Earnhardt raced onto the track one hour later, he didn't slow down to look at the tire marks on the asphalt or the black paint on the wall. He just drove harder. "I don't know if I can ever go through that turn without thinking of Neil," he said. "It would be disrespectful to him if I didn't. But I also know that it would piss Bonnett off if I lost a race out there because I was getting all emotional."

Now none of us can look at 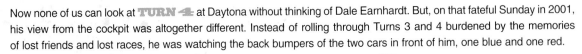 TURN 4 at Daytona without thinking of Dale Earnhardt. But, on that fateful Sunday in 2001, his view from the cockpit was altogether different. Instead of rolling through Turns 3 and 4 burdened by the memories of lost friends and lost races, he was watching the back bumpers of the two cars in front of him, one blue and one red.

IN THE MOMENTS BEFORE HE CLOSED OUT HIS LIFE ON THE BIGGEST STAGE IN STOCK CAR RACING,

HE GAZED DOWN THE TRACK INTO THE SUN. THE TWO CARS FORGED AHEAD. ONE WAS DRIVEN BY MICHAEL WALTRIP, THE OTHER BY DALE EARNHARDT JR. AS THEY STREAKED ACROSS THE FINISH LINE, BOTH BORE THE BLACK AND RED LOGO OF DALE EARNHARDT INC.

TAKE THAT, YOU SON OF A GUN.

CHAPTER

HE IS KNIT TIGHTLY INTO THE LORE OF OUR COUNTRY NOW, IMMORTALIZED IN POETRY AND SONG. HIS FACE APPEARS ON A POSTAGE STAMP, A SILVER DOLLAR, AND A MONOPOLY BOARD. IN FACT, YOU CAN SPEND NEARLY AN ETERNITY BASKING IN HIS GLORY . . . ON T-SHIRTS, WATCHES, BASEBALL CAPS, CHARCOAL, SOFT DRINK CANS, SUNTAN LOTION, TOY TRAINS, HAND TOOLS, CLOCKS, KEY CHAINS, BUMPER STICKERS, BELT BUCKLES, COOKIES, ICE CREAM SANDWICHES, SUNGLASSES, SOCKS, SWEATSHIRTS, HATS, SUSPENDERS, CHAIRS, BEDSHEETS, EAR-RINGS, PINS, VENDING MACHINES, AND $1,500 LAMBSKIN LEATHER JACKETS. HIS REACH IS SO VAST THAT PEOPLE HAVE TAKEN TO COMPARING HIM TO ELVIS. SO WHAT IS IT ABOUT THIS MAN, THE INTIMIDATOR, THAT PEOPLE FIND SO APPEALING? WHY IS IT THAT HIS STORY RESONATES SO DEEPLY IN OUR HEARTS?

WELL, FOR STARTERS, HE WALKED WITH US MERE MORTALS. "HE WAS WHAT EVERY GUY WANTS TO BE," CHOCOLATE MYERS TOLD AUTHOR RICHARD ERNSBERGER, "A REGULAR GUY—UNTIL YOU PUT HIM IN A RACE CAR."

Indeed, there is something supremely gratifying about Earnhardt's rags-to-riches success. He was the boy from Kannapolis who conquered the world, the ninth-grade dropout who fought his way to the top with pluck and perseverance. He lived his life as most men do. He rose with the sun and put in an honest day's work. When he wasn't racing, he was cleaning the barn or pulling tree stumps from the yard on his tractor. Long after he had made his fortune, he held fast to his roots. He knew the price of a carton of milk. He shopped at the local hardware store. And he always raced like he was chasing the rent money. He built his empire not twenty miles from his childhood home—the one with the rockers on the front porch.

HE WAS REBEL TO THE CORE. MOCKING THOSE WHO BRISTLED AT THE ROUGH-AND-TUMBLE REALITIES OF HIS SPORT. "THIS ISN'T TENNIS," HE SNARLED.

HE WAS

IF YOU SPRAINED YOUR FINGER, HE PULLED IT. IF YOU CHANGED THE RULES, HE FELT COMPELLED TO BREAK THEM—ALL IN GOOD CLEAN FUN, OF COURSE. AS A FELLOW RACER ONCE REMARKED, EARNHARDT COULD GIVE AN ASPIRIN A HEADACHE.

EARNHARDT HIMSELF DID NOT DISPUTE THAT FACT, BUT HE ONLY BULLIED THOSE WITH THE MEANS TO DEFEND THEM-SELVES, NEVER THOSE WHO WERE LESS FORTUNATE. THERE'S AN IMPORTANT DISTINCTION THERE—ONE THAT CORPORATE AMERICA WELL UNDERSTOOD. AFTER ALL, IT WAS GM GOODWRENCH THAT PURCHASED THE INTIMIDATOR IMAGE, GM GOODWRENCH THAT BUFFED IT TO A GLOWING SHEEN. THAT SLEEK BLACK CHARIOT WITH THE NUMBER 3 NOSING INTO THE WIND WAS AN EXPERTLY DESIGNED BUSINESS CARD FOR THE COMPANY'S STAR SPOKESMAN: PART DARTH VADER, PART OAKLAND RAIDER, PART JOHNNY CASH. MAKE NO MISTAKE, HOWEVER, EARNHARDT HAD THE GOODS TO SELL IT.

// DALE EARNHARDT AND BILL ELLIOTT
ROLL DURING AN ACCIDENT IN LAP 142
OF THE 1998 DIE HARD 500 AT TALLADEGA
SUPERSPEEDWAY.

LIKE ANY GREAT SUPER-HERO, HE HAD MOMENTS OF WEAKNESS, BUT

HE NEVER LET THEM DEFEAT HIM.

A BONA FIDE WARRIOR, HE RETURNED TO FIGHT EACH DAY.

HE ONCE WON A RACE WHILE HAULING THE CARCASS OF A BATTERED CAR ON HIS ROOFTOP. AT BRISTOL IN 1985, HE LOST HIS POWER STEERING IN THE FIRST HOUR OF A RACE. HE WRESTLED THE CAR AROUND THE TRACK FOR 400 LAPS TO WIN. AT ONTARIO MOTOR SPEEDWAY IN 1980, HE CHARGED ONTO THE BLACKTOP FROM THE PITS WITH ONLY TWO OF FIVE LUG NUTS ON HIS RIGHT REAR WHEEL. HE GUTTED OUT THREE HAIR-RAISING LAPS BEFORE NASCAR OFFICIALS ORDERED HIM BACK TO PIT ROAD. HE FINISHED FIFTH, EDGING OUT CALE YARBOROUGH FOR THAT FIRST WINSTON CUP CHAMPIONSHIP.

OVER THE YEARS, EARNHARDT RACED WITH A **BROKEN STERNUM, BROKEN COLLARBONES, BROKEN RIBS, AND A BROKEN KNEECAP.** *HE FOUGHT OFF THE PAIN FOR 648 CONSECUTIVE STARTS.*

HIS THIRST FOR VICTORY WAS THAT STRONG.

ONE YEAR AT CHARLOTTE HE WAS RACING SEVENTH WITH A FEW LAPS TO GO WHEN THE CAUTION FLAG CAME OUT. CHOCOLATE MYERS RADIOED TO TELL HIM TO STAY ON THE TRACK, TAKE THE TOP-TEN FINISH. EARNHARDT RADIOED RIGHT BACK. "BOYS, I'M COMIN' DOWN PIT ROAD. I DIDN'T COME HERE TO FINISH IN THE TOP TEN. I CAME HERE TO WIN."

HE'D DO ALMOST ANYTHING TO ACHIEVE HIS GOALS.

HE WILLINGLY ACCEPTED THE REPERCUSSIONS. EVEN NEIL BONNETT ONCE SAID,

"IF I CAN EVER CATCH HIM, I'M GOING TO PUNCH THE [CRAP] OUT OF HIM."

RICHARD PETTY—THE KING—WAS FAR MORE OMINOUS. IN 1987, HE TOLD *SPORTS ILLUSTRATED*, "THERE'LL COME A SUNDAY WHEN THERE WON'T BE ENOUGH WRECKERS TO PICK UP THE PIECES OF HIS CAR." THAT DAY NEVER CAME. ON THE OCCASION OF HIS LONE DAYTONA 500 VICTORY, EARNHARDT WAS SHOWERED WITH LOVE FROM ONE END OF PIT ROAD TO THE OTHER. BY THEN, HE WAS EVERYBODY'S ALL AMERICAN.

HE EMBODIED THE DRIVING SPIRIT OF THE NATION, THE FRONTIER MENTALITY OF THE WILD WEST

"I don't sit there and analyze things," he said. "I go out and make 'em happen." He was also a son of the South, a good ole boy with charm to spare, and a hero on Wall Street, a star-spangled champion of the free-market system. And what could be more heroic in Detroit than a man who stoops to conquer in his automobile—the kind of car you find parked in driveways all across the heartland?

IN AN AGE OF CONTROVERSIAL SPORTS FIGURES, DALE EARNHARDT WAS DEPENDABLE. HE DID NOT HOLD OUT. HE DID NOT STRIKE. HE DID NOT DANCE AND PREEN FOR THE CAMERA. HE SIMPLY PUT HIS HEAD DOWN AND DROVE LIKE THE DEVIL. HE KICKED AND SCRATCHED AND CLAWED HIS WAY TO THE FINISH AS IF HIS LIFE DEPENDED ON IT.

That's not to say that he did not make the most of TV. He arrived on the scene at the dawn of NASCAR's modern era and promptly stole the show, refusing to surrender it for more than twenty years. The fawning glow of the camera lens was there to record his every highlight. The Pass in the Grass, the astonishing thread-the-needle move at Bristol. As if by magic, the drama of his life always seemed to play out on the glittery asphalt of Daytona.

And yet, there is nothing false about his story. He was truly an American original. The outlaw's smile, the Southern charm, the car, the shades, the mustache: he made them all his own. We seem to have an unhealthy infatuation with numbers these days: triple doubles, home runs, thousand-yard seasons. Earnhardt did not need such figures to make his case. He relied on his actions.

FIVE DRIVERS IN NASCAR HISTORY HAVE MORE WINS. BET YOU CAN'T NAME THEM.

WHY?

BECAUSE APART FROM SEVEN-TIME WINSTON CUP CHAMPION RICHARD PETTY, THEIR RECORDS ARE INDISTIN-GUISHABLE.

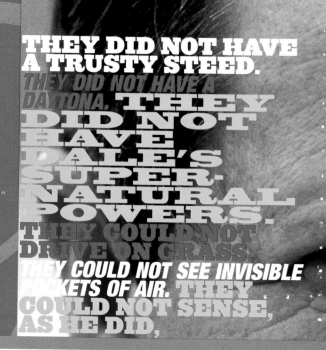

THEY DID NOT HAVE A TRUSTY STEED. THEY DID NOT HAVE A DAYTONA. THEY DID NOT HAVE DALE'S SUPER-NATURAL POWERS. THEY COULD NOT DRIVE ON GRASS. THEY COULD NOT SEE INVISIBLE POCKETS OF AIR. THEY COULD NOT SENSE, AS HE DID,

THE SLIGHTEST TREMOR IN A FULLY REVVED ENGINE.

AFTER AN UNEVENTFUL PRACTICE RUN AT BRISTOL ONE AFTERNOON, HE INFORMED HIS CREW THAT THE CAR'S CRANKSHAFT WAS BROKEN. HOW DID HE KNOW THIS, ASKED CHOCOLATE MYERS. THE CREWMAN HAD SEEN NOTHING IN THE HANDLING OF OLD NUMBER 3 TO SUGGEST A PROBLEM. "EASY," SAID EARNHARDT. "MY DAD USED TO MAKE ME DRIVE WEARING REAL THIN-SOLED SHOES SO I COULD FEEL THE MOTOR." SURE ENOUGH, HE WAS RIGHT: THE CRANKSHAFT NEEDED REPLACING.

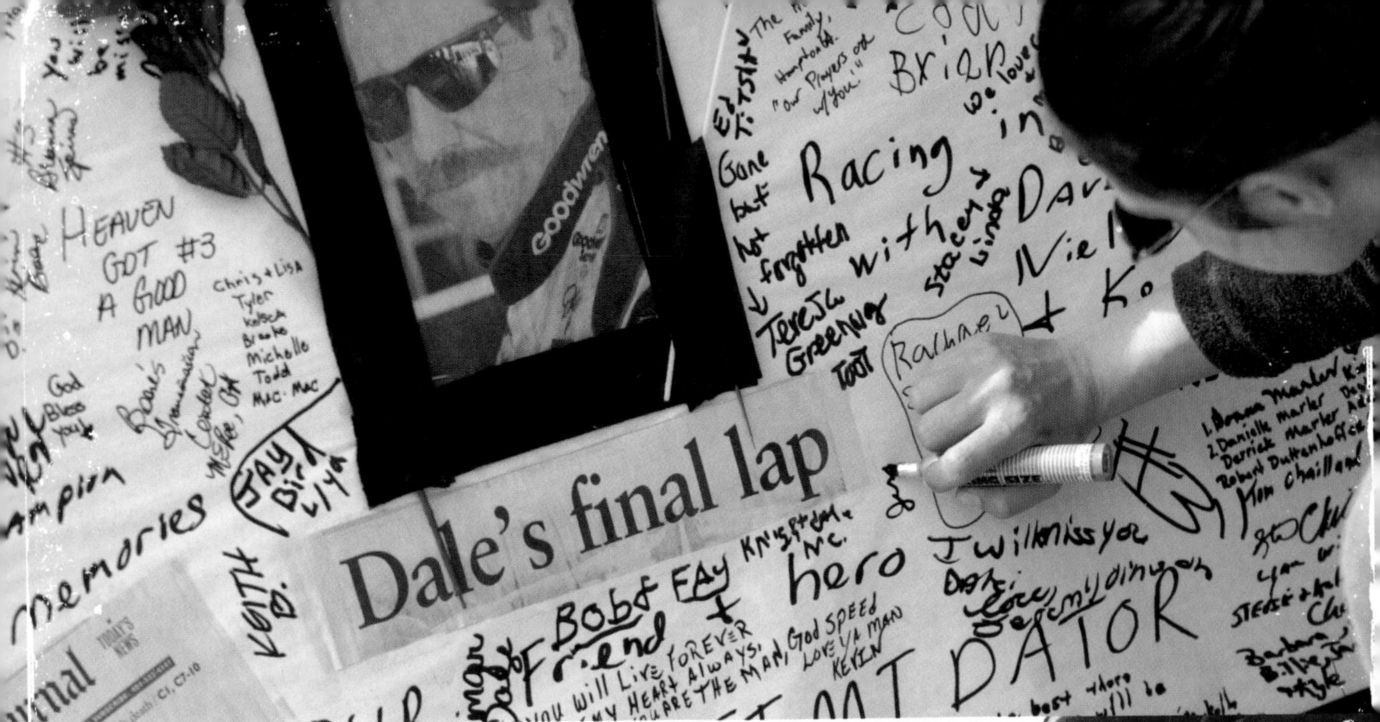

HEAVEN
GOT #3
A GOOD
MAN

Dale's final lap

Racing

hero

SO WHO'S TO SAY HE DID NOT STAND TEN FEET TALL?

HE CONQUERED EVERY-THING IN HIS PATH.

POVERTY. LACK OF EDUCATION. THE EVIL SPIRITS OF DAYTONA. WHEN HE ABSOLUTELY HAD TO WIN, HE WAS UNSTOPPABLE. HE TOOK HIS LICKS AND KEPT ON COMING. HE CARTWHEELED DOWN THE FRONT STRETCH AT TALLADEGA, PULLED HIMSELF FROM HIS SMOLDERING VEHICLE, AND WALKED TO THE AMBULANCE. HE BOLTED FROM AN AMBULANCE IN DAYTONA TO RETURN TO HIS BEAT-UP CAR. IN A WAY, IT ALMOST SEEMS THAT HE WAS DESTINED TO DIE ON THE LAST TURN OF THE LAST LAP AT DAYTONA.

WHAT MORE DID HE HAVE TO PROVE?

WE'LL MISS Y
DALE

IN THE END, DALE EARNHARDT IS SO MUCH MORE THAN ELVIS. HE IS JAMES DEAN AND DANIEL BOONE AND HUCK FINN AND DIRTY HARRY. HE IS BONNIE AND CLYDE AND GENERAL LEE AND JOHN WAYNE AND ROBIN HOOD. HE IS MORE THAN HUMAN. HE IS DIVINE INSPIRATION. THAT IS WHY A MAN IN OHIO WINS THE LOTTERY AND IMMEDIATELY SETS HIMSELF TO BUILDING A WORLD-CLASS COLLECTION OF EARNHARDT MEMORABILIA, WHY PEOPLE IN FLORIDA SEE THE NUMBER 3 ON THE SIDE OF A GOAT, WHY DECALS BEARING THE REAL NUMBER 3 APPEAR TO THIS DAY ON BUMPERS IN THE FAR NORTHERN REACHES OF CANADA. IT IS WHY PEOPLE STILL GATHER BY THE THOUSANDS TO CELEBRATE HIS BIRTHDAY.

HE IS SO MUCH MORE THAN A MAN. **HE IS A LEGEND.**

EARNHARDT'S LEGIONS OF FANS HAVE FOUND EXTRAORDINARY WAYS TO SHOW THEIR DEVOTION.

CLOCKWISE FROM UPPER LEFT
// A WOMAN IN LIVONIA, MICHIGAN, BUILDS A GARDEN FOR CHARITY WITH FLOWER-PATCH REPLICAS OF NASCAR TRACKS // A GOAT ON A FLORIDA FARM BEARS THE MAGIC NUMBER 3 // FANS MOURN DALE'S PASSING // A CANDLE LIT BY A MAKESHIFT MEMORIAL // THE STATUE OF DALE AT DAYTONA INTERNATIONAL SPEEDWAY // A CAT NAMED ROMEO BEARS THE MARK OF 3 IN DELAND, FLORIDA // A SOUVENIR 3 FLAG FLIES UNDER THE STARS AND STRIPES AT A TAILGATE RALLY // A FAN AND HIS THIRTEEN-YEAR OLD DOG NEVER MISSED A SINGLE EARNHARDT RACE

ACKNOWLEDGMENTS

MUCH OF THE MATERIAL IN THIS BOOK WAS CULLED FROM RESEARCH AND INTERVIEWS CONDUCTED BY ESPN REPORTERS. HOWEVER, THE AUTHOR COULD NOT HAVE PAINTED A COMPLETE PORTRAIT OF DALE EARNHARDT WITHOUT USING QUOTES, ANECDOTES, AND PERSONAL RECOLLECTIONS PROVIDED BY THE MANY FINE WRITERS WHO CHRONICLED THE DRIVER'S LIFE. IN PARTICULAR, ESPN BOOKS IS INDEBTED TO RICHARD ERNSBERGER JR., AUTHOR OF *GOD, PEPSI, AND GROOVIN' ON THE HIGH SIDE: TALES FROM THE NASCAR CIRCUIT*; TOM GILLISPIE, AUTHOR OF *I REMEMBER DALE EARNHARDT: MEMORIES OF AND TESTIMONIALS TO STOCK CAR RACING'S MOST BELOVED DRIVER, AS TOLD BY THE PEOPLE WHO KNEW HIM BEST*; JONATHAN INGRAM, AUTHOR OF *DALE EARNHARDT*; LEIGH MONTVILLE, AUTHOR OF *AT THE ALTAR OF SPEED: THE FAST LIFE AND TRAGIC DEATH OF DALE EARNHARDT*; AND RICH WOLFE, AUTHOR OF *REMEMBERING DALE EARNHARDT: WONDERFUL STORIES CELEBRATING THE LIFE OF RACING'S GREATEST DRIVER*. WE ALSO EXTEND OUR GRATITUDE TO THE REPORTERS OF *THE CHARLOTTE OBSERVER, CIRCLE TRACK, NASCAR SCENE, THE SALISBURY (NORTH CAROLINA) POST, SPORTS ILLUSTRATED, STOCK CAR RACING, SUNBELT VIDEO,* AND *THE EARNHARDT LEGACY*. THE SCOPE AND IMAGINATION OF THIS PROJECT WOULD NOT BE POSSIBLE WITHOUT THE MANY THOUGHTFUL CONTRIBUTIONS OF MARK ASHENFELTER, ROBERT EISELE, KAREN GREENFELD, BURKE MAGNUS, J.B. MORRIS, DR. JERRY PUNCH, MICHAEL SOLOMON, TORI STEVENS, SIUNG TJIA, GRETCHEN YOUNG, AND CRAIG WINSTON.

A ROUNDTABLE PRESS BOOK

ALL RIGHTS RESERVED. NO PART OF THIS BOOK MAY BE USED OR REPRODUCED IN ANY MANNER WHATSOEVER WITHOUT THE WRITTEN PERMISSION OF THE PUBLISHER. PRINTED IN THE UNITES STATES OF AMERICA. FOR INFORMATION, ADDRESS: HYPERION, 77 WEST 66TH STREET, NEW YORK, NY 10023-6298. COPYRIGHT © 2004 ESPN, INC. ALL RIGHTS RESERVED.

ESPN BOOKS

EDITOR: CHRIS RAYMOND
PUBLISHING DIRECTOR: SANDY HOLMES DESHONG
RESEARCH: DARRELL TRIMBLE

ROUNDTABLE PRESS, INC.

DIRECTORS: JULIE MERBERG, MARSHA MELNICK
EXECUTIVE EDITOR: PATTY BROWN
EDITOR: JOHN GLENN
DESIGN: PLATINUM DESIGN, INC. NYC
ART DIRECTOR: MATTHEW BOULOUTIAN
TEXT: DAVID FISHER
PHOTO RESEARCH AND EDITING: DAMON DIMARCO

PHOTOGRAPHY CREDITS

CREDITS ARE INDICATED BY PAGE NUMBER AND LETTERS: FROM TOP TO BOTTOM, T STANDS FOR TOP, C FOR CENTER, AND B FOR BOTTOM. FROM LEFT TO RIGHT, L STANDS FOR LEFT, M FOR MIDDLE, AND R FOR RIGHT.

AP: WIDE WORLD IMAGES: 34–35; 54 (TR); 55(TL, TR); 63; 107 (T); 154 (TL, C2, C4, BR). © BETTMANN/CORBIS: 10 (BL); 80–81; 94 (INSET). © REUTERS/CORBIS: 154 (C1). CHARLOTTE OBSERVER: 10 (T); 49 (L); 87; 92 (B); 93; 94–95; 98 (TR); 106 (B); 107 (B); 112 (BR); 113 (B); 117 (B); 121; 124–125; 143 (TL); 152 (B); 154 (C3). ESPN: 154 (TR, BM). TRAVIS BELL/ESPN: 5 (TR); 18–19; 22 (T, C); 23 (T, BR); 24–25; 28 (TL). GETTY IMAGES: 38–39 (B); 54 (TL); 55 (TM); 126–127; 129; 132 (B); 142 (T); 147 (B); 152 (T). INTERNATIONAL MOTORSPORTS HALL OF FAME: BACK COVER (ML); 16; 20 (L, R); 21 (B); 22 (B); 23 (M, BL); 89; 99 (TR); 105 (B); 106 (T); 112 (TR); 113 (R); 149 (L). © MOTORSPORTS IMAGES AND ARCHIVES, INC.: 130–131 (T). JIM GUND/SPORTS ILLUSTRATED: BACK COVER (B); 123 (B); 128 (T); 132 (TL); 136; 137 (T); 139 (TL); 140; 143 (BR); 149 (R); 151. JOHN IACONO/SPORTS ILLUSTRATED: 76; 80 (TL); 84 (L); 85 (TL, TR). PAUL KENNEDY/SPORTS ILLUSTRATED: 79 (TR); 84 (R). NIGEL KINRADE/SPORTS ILLUSTRATED: 97 (TL); 100 (BL); 105 (TL); 118–119; 120 (B). HEINZ KLUETMEIER/SPORTS ILLUSTRATED: 37 (L). V. J. LOVERO/SPORTS ILLUSTRATED: 100 (BR). MANNY RUBIO/SPORTS ILLUSTRATED: 71 (CR); 73 (TR); 74 (TL); 79 (TL); 85 (B). KARIM SHAMSI-BASHA/SPORTS ILLUSTRATED: 38 (T); 144–145. GEORGE TIEDEMANN/SPORTS ILLUSTRATED: BACK COVER (MR); FRONT COVER (ALL); BACK COVER (CR); 1; 4–5 (BACKGROUND); 4 (B3, B5); 5 (B3, B4, BR); 8–9; 10 (BR); 32–33; 38–39 (M); 40–41; 44 (T, BR); 45 (B); 46–47; 56–57; 66 (T, B); 69; 71 (B); 72; 74–75; 77; 85 (M); 87 (T); 92 (T); 96–97 (BACKGROUND); 99 (TL); 100 (T); 101 (R); 102; 103; 110–111; 112 (TL); 114–115; 117 (T); 133; 134–135; 137 (BL, BR); 138–139 (BACKGROUND); 146–147 (BACKGROUND); 148 (B); 155. TONY TOMSIC/SPORTS ILLUSTRATED: 5 (B1, B2); 90–91; 98–99 (BACKGROUND); 108; 111 (BR). ALLEN KEE/WIREIMAGE.COM: 36 (TL); 37 (BR); 44 (L, TR); 45 (T); 49 (B, R); 60 (R); 79 (B); 154 (BL); 96 (TL); 97 (TR); 143 (BL, TR). JOE ROBBINS/WIREIMAGE.COM: 114 (BL). BRIAN A. WESTERHOLT/WIREIMAGE.COM: 146 (TL); 153.

ISBN 1-4013-4443-7

FIRST EDITION

2 4 6 8 10 9 7 5 3 1

ONE MAN. ONE SPORT. ONE NATION.

3

STARRING *BARRY PEPPER* AS
DALE EARNHARDT

On DVD December 14th

Own the first and only movie about Dale Earnhardt.
Includes a bonus disc of exclusive Earnhardt interviews and races.

Premieres Saturday, December 11th 9PMET on ESPN